Protect Yourself

Robert J. Disario

ISBN: 9781521308844

FOR LISA

The strongest woman I've ever met. Her compassion, dedication and strength were the inspiration for this book. It is often said God gives only what one can handle. Well, God didn't know what he was up against when he challenged Lisa.

CONTENTS

ACKNOWLEDGMENTS

This book could not have been possible without the support of my friends and family. Their support and encouragement motivate me to keep writing for the fun of it. Also, a big thank you to all my Facebook friends who helped to make #Nationwide Police Strike a number one best seller on Amazon in August, 2016.

INTRODUCTION

At one point in your life you'll find yourself victimized by your fellow man. That's just a simple fact. Victimization can range from damage to your car or home, or theft of your personal possessions. You may also become a victim of the worst type of offense: violent crime. Unfortunately, in our society it's not a question of if, but when. This book is intended to provide tips and tricks for protecting yourself from the most common types of victimization. Also included are steps to avoid becoming a victim of not-so common types of crime.

My earliest memory of being victimized was when my bike was stolen out of my friend's backyard. I thought my world was coming to an end. At the tender age of ten, my bike was my most important possession. In retrospect, I realize that the theft of my bicycle was my own fault. Subconsciously, I trusted society and its inhabitants to leave my property alone. I wrongly assumed that my unsecured bike would be there when I returned – childhood innocence at its best. Unfortunately, many grown adults follow this premise. They lead their lives with blinders on with respect to society's criminals – criminals who prey on the vulnerable, the weak or those who aren't prepared to protect themselves.

Today, we live in a society where the need for physical safety could not be more important. Society requires us to make a conscious effort to pay closer attention to our security, as both Americans and human beings. It is my strong contention that at the end of the day, you and you alone are responsible for your own safety. This bears repeating: YOU and YOU ALONE are responsible for your safety. Unfortunately, Americans have become too dependent on both the government and technology to provide protection. In reality, many people have relinquished total security control to others. When the neighbors play loud music, we call the police (government). When the neighbor's home gets burglarized, we install a house alarm (technology).

This was never the purpose of government in either a municipality, state or federal capacity.

For example, there are more than 770,000 police officers in the United States and another million or so federal state and municipal first responders. This includes the U.S. Border Patrol, INS, ICE, Secret Service, FBI, Intelligence community, DEA, etc. These agencies, while helpful in a broader scale with respect to protection against foreign entities, do nothing for me in a parking garage in East St. Louis. Even though the local police are doing everything they can, patrolling, investigating past crimes, etc., there's little they can do in the split second during which I get grabbed from behind and tossed into a van. I realize this is an extreme example, but I use it only to illustrate my point.

Thus, we need to take individual ownership of our own safety. Humans are animals with the luxury of free will (and opposable thumbs). While most of us use our free will for good, criminals will feed on others even if it benefits them only temporarily.

I work as a police officer in an urban setting. Much of my time is spent patrolling, following up on past crimes and creating a visible deterrence. It's in this capacity that I see people first hand avoiding the elephant in the room. They remain occupied, completely distracted from the criminality of human life – criminality that is all around them and that they choose to avoid. People of all ages, all genders, walking down the street with their faces fixed on their cell phones. People waiting for the bus, walking down the street or in line at a fast food restaurant, completely oblivious to their surroundings. These people have relinquished control of their safety to others. Control is left to both those who are paid to provide safety (police) as well as to those who surround them. They communicate to their fellow man a level of trust that is undeserved and completely careless.

Hopefully, by reading this book and becoming a #PY student, you'll begin to prepare your brain and create a mindset ready to defend yourself at any moment.

This man has stopped in the middle of the sidewalk to communicate using his phone. Completely oblivious to his radius he's a prime target.

I don't profess to be an expert in anything other than being a trained, professional observer. I've been a police officer since 2001 and investigated thousands of crimes. Throughout my career, I have paid particular attention to answering the question *why?* Why was this person chosen to be a victim? What makes them different from any other person? Many times, I've found a simple and logical answer. At other times, there is no answer and the victim was as random as human life.

For example, several years ago I was working the overnight shift when our dispatch center received a call of a home invasion that had just occurred in an apartment building. For those who don't know, a home invasion is where the suspect enters a home while being armed or becoming armed with the intent to hurt the occupants. The building they chose was a nondescript brownstone probably built in the early 1900's. What immediately struck me as odd was that each building in the row of brownstones looked exactly alike and consisted of about six apartments within each section. At the time I received the call, the crime appeared to be random. However, as we obtained more information, got a look inside the apartment and spoke to the dummy occupants, it became clear within the first twenty minutes or so that these guys were drug dealers and had been targeted for the drug money. Simple.

Conversely, I had a call of a suspect who had run up to a couple that had just left the local movie theater and punched the man in the face. The victim said there was no interaction with the suspect beforehand and he had never seen the man before. Random. When I caught up to the suspect (whom I knew well in the neighborhood), his explanation as to why he had committed this violent crime was because the victim didn't deserve his female companion. Needless to say, he suffered from mental health issues that caused him to be outwardly aggressive to strangers.

Answering the question *why* can be a difficult venture. However, just as these two examples prove, if we explore the *why*, we can begin to address the *how*. *How* do I protect myself from becoming a victim?

In the following chapters I will attempt to answer both these questions while providing tips and tricks for taking common-sense, proactive steps to protect yourself. Many of these tips you already know, and some you don't. Some you'll suggest are so common sense that not doing them borders on idiotic. But let me assure you, if it's included in this book, someone I have dealt with became a victim because they did it and made no effort to protect themselves. If, by the end of this book, you apply even one tip or trick to your everyday life I'll call that a win!

#PY Tip: In each chapter, you'll see these tips with an explanation and example of how they work or may work.

#PY Exercise: You may also see this, which offers a field exercise you can do in your daily life to get yourself out of your comfort zone!

CHAPTER TWO
SITUATIONAL AWARENESS

The concept of situational awareness has been taught in military and law enforcement communities for years. It's the idea that you are constantly aware of your immediate surroundings or "situation." However, I don't care for this phrase because the term *situation* gives the impression that you're currently involved in some sort of event or occurrence.

For example, you're on a mission to storm a castle protected by armed guards. Your senses are heightened and you're aware of your "situation." Most of us will never become engaged in this type of sorcery. Thus, the term *situation awareness* is not applicable. The situation I want to discuss and will refer to in this book is everyday existence. As human beings and Americans, we are merely traveling through this mission we call life. We make our way to the train, then across town to work and back again. On the weekends, we travel to the zoo with our kids and occasionally out to eat at a restaurant. This is the mission we're all on. Thus, I will replace the term *situation awareness* with the term *radius awareness*.

I want every reader to re-enter the world aware of their immediate radius. I'm not concerned about what's happening on the other side of the world or even on the other side of the street. I'm concerned about what's happening in front, beside and most importantly behind you. That's it. If you can control this space you'll have a head start in protecting yourself.

The idea of radius awareness is a human instinct that's in common practice across the world. Every police officer who has attended a police academy in the United states exercises this practice every hour of every day. My purpose is to deliver this concept to the masses. I developed radius awareness after watching people unnecessarily become victims. They exist amongst the enemy with blinders on. Their heads are buried in their phones, which diverts their attention and causes them to turn their backs to the enemy. Many don't face the enemy because they appear undesirable or threatening. They avoid eye contact so as not to poke the bear. Why do we do that? Why do we silence the little voice in our heads that shouts

"Danger, danger?" The answer is simple: We don't want to be rude. That's it, folks. I wish I had a more scientific explanation for why we're not listening to our animal instincts but that's it.

Most people know what they're doing is wrong. They know that the guy staring at them at the subway station is a menace and poses a significant threat. We all have this voice inside our heads that says "Danger, danger!" The hair on the back of your neck stands up and you get the feeling that "something is just not right!" But we commonly silence this voice, this gut instinct, for fear of being rude to another person.

In essence, we're rolling the dice with our safety in the interest of maintaining societal norms.

When you were little, your mom told you to smile and be nice. I find myself saying to my son all the time, "Be nice, Dominic. Don't be rude." And it's true, most times we should be nice. But there are times when you need to be rude (sorry, Mom).

Let's take *Subway Jimmy* as an example. Subway Jimmy is standing on the platform of the train station. He's leaning against the pillar and he has eyes only for you. He creeps you out. You avert your eyes and pretend not to see him for fear you'll poke the bear. Thus, you return to Words with Friends or some other pastime, patiently waiting for your train. While you're minding your own business, he's sizing you up. He's calculating whether you're vulnerable enough to take advantage of. Now, this can be for either monetary profit (e.g., robbery) or urge gratification (e.g., rape, sexual assault). Either way, you're a target. You've demonstrated to him that you're unaware of your surroundings and that he'll have the upper hand when he strikes. If he does rob you, he knows you won't be able to describe him because you avoided eye contact at all costs (thanks, Mom).

Now let's say you enter the platform and take a quick scan of your radius. You see Subway Jimmy and a couple other people already boarding the train. You take a quick eye-shot of Subway Jimmy and see he's wearing blue jeans and 90's grunge flannel. You then walk to your side of the platform but instead of turning your back to Subway Jimmy, you blade your body at an angle so that your right shoulder is facing him. Instead of scrolling Facebook, you keep your phone in your pocket and take a quick scan of your immediate surroundings.

Out of these two descriptions, who is more likely to be a victim? Yeah, there are those people who, no matter what the victim does, will strike; I talk more about types of criminals in an upcoming chapter. Let me tell you something, though; if Subway Jimmy makes even the slightest move toward the second victim, that person would be ready. Their senses are already heightened, their body is bladed so that the reaction time is quicker and their phone is not creating a barrier to self-defense.

So, let's talk specifically about radius awareness. One should be aware and overly protective of their immediate surrounds for up to three feet. That's right, draw an invisible circle around your body with a diameter of six feet (or a radius of three feet). This area is your area of concentration. Those who come into this area are classified into three categories: those just passing through, those we let in or those who are violators. We must protect ourselves from those who violate and invade this area. Often, this is unavoidable. If you're on the train during morning rush hour, there's nothing you can do about the guy rubbing up against you (sorry). However, in normal, everyday activity, there's something you can do.

Next, we must be able to take quick eye-shots of the area outside our radius. What is an eye-shot? Think of it as a Google Maps camera that drives around the street, constantly taking pictures. You want to take a quick shot and look away. You will collect a lot of data in that split second; however, you don't need to remember all of it. You just need to be exposed to it and fit it into one of two categories: threat and not a threat. Please don't worry about judging a book by its cover, or passing judgment on your fellow man (wah, wah). This is an action completed by your body, not your brain. Your instinct will tell you which is which and communicate it physiologically.

Crime knows no sex, race, color, status, ethnicity or religious beliefs – we are all fair game. For this reason, the hair on the back of your neck and the pit in your stomach will inform you about the threat. To form an evaluation, however, you must provide your body with the data. If you starve your body of that valuable information, it can't make informed decisions – decisions that WILL save your life.

Let's say, for example, you're standing in line at Dunkin Donuts. (Yes, I love DD's and since the advent of Order-On-The-Go, this is something I never do anymore.) Nonetheless, you can sense the guy behind you in line invading your radius. Whatever you do, do not silence this feeling; embrace it! The first line of defense is an eye-shot. Collect the data and process it. If your initial sense is right, you need to act. Since you're in line for a coffee, your movement is limited. In this situation, I would first attempt the perpendicular turn. This defense mechanism calls for the body to be turned in such a way that your shoulder (not your back) is now facing him. If Creepy Jim had intentions to pick my pocket (or purse), it's now out of his reach.

Conversely, you may find yourself in a situation where there's ample space. When Creepy Jim invades your radius, you can begin the retreat procedure. This is where you simply take a half step away from Creepy Jim. It's a reaction our bodies have naturally and is commonly referred to as *fight or flight*. Adults tend to suppress this natural reaction for fear of being rude. However, I embrace it. When Creepy Jim closes the distance after my "flight," that's when I "fight." However, instead of fighting, I may extend my elbow ever so slightly so that I bump Creepy Jim. This may do one of two things: either he realizes he's gotten too close and moves of his own accord or I do it hard enough (maybe a second time) that it forces him away. Now remember, I don't want to pick a fight with Creepy Jim, but I need to protect my radius.

In spite of your attempt to maintain your radius, friendly people violate it and speak to you up close. In our society, it shows respect to approach another person, look them in the eye and address them. In your average, everyday interaction with a fellow human, this is acceptable. We allow them in temporarily. However, when someone invades your radius, you must be protective of your space. Most times people will understand if you calmly take a step back but you can also raise your hand about chest high with your fingers lightly touching the person. If you can smile and nod your head, they'll get the point. If, after you step back, they continue to approach, you could interpret that as a sign of aggression. This does not mean you need to have a battle on the street, but you can offer a friendly reminder not to stand too close to you. Usually this works and the person will apologize. If Creepy Jim continues his approach, this is when you can go hands on by using a *distance maker* and screw.

Every Door is a Threat

Often while I'm working as a police officer, I visit a local restaurant to eat my lunch or dinner. Unfortunately, police officers who work the street do not have the convenience of a kitchenette or even a fridge to keep their sandwiches cold. Therefore, we are forced to go to the local sub shop for a quick sandwich and eat in the "dining room." Even though I'm taking a break to eat, the fact remains that I'm still in uniform and a potential target.

In November 2009, the law enforcement community suffered a blow when three of our brothers and one sister were killed while they sat in a local coffee shop just outside Tacoma, Washington. This incident illustrates why the following techniques are so important. When a police officer sits in a public place, like a restaurant, she must sit with her back against the wall and facing the entry. This is for two reasons. The first reason is that you can see whether any patrons already in the establishment are going to attack. If your back is against the wall, there is no way they can attack without your seeing the threat and protecting yourself. Second, while facing the entry, you may be able to see an attack entering the restaurant.

As a #PY student, you must be on the lookout for anybody looking suspicious as they walk in. Signs of someone who is suspicious: eyes darting from side to side; apparent nervousness; hands in pockets and clutching something; heavy clothing in warmer temperatures; donning a ski cap or other head cover as they walk in. My worst fear is that I'll be in a local establishment and a robber will come through the door and get the upper hand. Once you understand its importance, you will do it every day. I've positioned myself in public places for so long, my wife now knows where I'm going to want to sit when we get to our table. Who knew?

#PY Tip: The following is an excerpt from my upcoming book, *Becoming a Police Officer*. It illustrates a very important technique that police officers employ every day to keep safe.

What types of body techniques can we employ to protect ourselves while doing our job? One technique that is stressed in the academy is keeping your hands above your waist. This may be difficult to imagine, so watch your evening news to get a better idea of what I'm talking about. News reporters and anchormen apply this technique because it looks better on television than having their arms dangling like salami.

Police officers, on the other hand, use this technique not because it looks better but because it is a defense mechanism. If you keep your hands about stomach high, without interlacing your fingers, you will be able to raise your hands quicker to defend an impending blow to the face or head. Both hands can be brought up to your face extremely fast to block a punching hand or thrown weapon. Once the threat is blocked, you can immediately spring into a strike of your choice. The strike can be a heel-palm strike, a front punch or a push off to create distance (distance maker) *and transition to a tool such as the baton or O.C. spray. When my hands are in this position, I usually spin my wedding band so that it looks a little more casual. My theory behind looking casual is that the more casual I appear, the less offensive the person to whom I am speaking may perceive my actions to be. One may become offended if they knew that as you spoke to them, you kept your hands in a defensive posture. This may cause a breakdown in the ever-important communication process. If you're casual and less obvious, most of the time people will not even notice you're doing it.*

#PY Exercise: Begin practicing your radius awareness today. Next time you're out in public, conduct a sweep of your surroundings. Take a couple eye-shots and see who else is paying attention. Make eye contact and assess your surroundings. Chances are, nobody even looks up from their screens. Pay particular attention to anybody invading your radius and begin the retreat procedure. Is it comfortable?

CHAPTER THREE
OPPORTUNITY BASED CRIME VS. PREMEDITATED CRIME

A common theme you'll see throughout this book is whether victimization was the result of opportunity or, instead, was premeditated. This is very important because we want to protect ourselves from both. We must take steps to prevent the opportunity and lessen the effects of those premeditated crimes against us.

Presentation: How do you present yourself in public? Do you stare off into space while waiting for the bus? Do you check your email while walking from your car to the coffee shop? Or are you focused on those who enter your radius, constantly sizing them up and determining whether they're a threat? This exercise requires a little self-analysis. You will have to look introspectively and subjectively at the way you present yourself. Are you welcoming an attack just by the way you sit, walk or stand?

Along these lines, how do you present your home on a day-to-day basis? Does your home communicate to potential intruders that it's protected? When you're at work during the day, does your home look vacant? Does your home scream "valuables inside"?

Let's discuss opportunity-based crime, or OBC. OBC is where a criminal observes a situation and ponders whether, if he acts upon the presented opportunity, he'll get away with it. Will his actions benefit his situation? This is a very basic example of immediate gratification crime.

The criminal is walking out of the restroom of the coffee shop (which is common amongst undesirables who visit local establishments and don't buy anything) and sees a purse hanging on the back of a chair. As he walks out, he slips his hand right under the strap, and onto his shoulder it goes. It's so smooth, even those who may see the motion don't realize they've just witnessed a crime. That is OBC. Another example is the homeless guy who walks down the street checking car door handles. This is another smooth skill that is unobservable by most who see it. As he pulls on the handle, he checks whether the door opens. If it does, he reaches in and grabs whatever he can fit into his pockets: change, iPods, cell phone chargers, etc.

Premeditated crime is just the opposite. This is the murder for hire in which the criminal develops a plan to get the victim alone and kill him, or the white-collar criminal who opens a bank account under a fictitious name and siphons the customers' money a little at a time.

The only element that differentiates these two types of crime is the planning. Did I plan to grab the purse or did I just see the opportunity and strike? Did I lure my wife to the woods to kill and bury her or did I catch her cheating with my best friend and snap? There may be some overlap but essentially that's the difference.

#PY Exercise: The next time you find yourself in public, try to step out of your body and observe what you're doing. What is your posture? Did you see that guy approach and stand behind you? Are your hands buried in your jacket or could they defend you during an immediate attack?

A man sits on a bench completely disregarding his radius. His attention and mind is consumed by his electronic device.

CHAPTER FOUR
TYPES OF VICTIMS

I'm a simple learner. To understand anything, I break the data into small groups for simplicity. Thus, victims can be broken down into three groups. The first group contains those who take necessary precautions to protect themselves. These are the people who bubble wrap their kids and don't leave home. I call them Group 1ers. These people are constantly on high alert. They have alarms on their homes and bars on their windows. They lock the windows on the second floor and constantly worry that they're not doing enough. This group consists of about five percent of the American population. I'd be surprised if you even know one of these people.

The second group is the person on the other end of the spectrum. This person puts themselves into situations in which they're more likely to be victimized. These are the people who go to raves and clubs without a care in the world. They take drinks and rides from strangers with an undeserved confidence in the goodness of society. If you do know one of these people, you constantly ask yourself how it is that they're not victimized more often. Not that you mean them any harm – far from it. They simply put themselves into situations and provide opportunity for criminals. This group represents about five percent of the population as well.

The last group is everybody else. We make a really good effort to secure our homes and watch where we go and how we get there, but we still have a lot of work to do. This group represents about ninety percent of the American population. Chances are, if you're reading this book, you fall into this group. We occasionally drop our guard at the worst times and run the risk of being taken advantage of. But there is one commonality among all Group 3ers: the desire to not be rude.

As introduced in the previous chapter, our sense of politeness is stifling our human need to protect ourselves. On top of that is our undeserved faith in our fellow man. As a police officer, I feel as though every day I'm taking calls for a purse or laptop stolen from a Starbucks. I can literally write the report before I talk to the victim:

“I put my stuff down on the table, heard my name called and got up to grab my double mocha latte…(yada yada). When I got back to my table, my purse was gone...it was hanging on the back of my chair!”

So the story goes. People's faith in strangers gets them victimized more often than anything else. Add to that the fact that many others live in bubbles, but we’ll discuss that later.

Yes, I’d like to think that should I leave my jacket or gym bag at my table and go to the lavatory, it’ll be there when I return. But the simple fact is, there’s no guarantee. So, what does this have to do with the type of victim category you fall into? Its huge! If you want to practice good #PY habits and minimize your risk of victimization, you need to recondition your mind. Recondition your way of thinking so that every situation is a threat and every stranger is not to be trusted.

Does this mean you have to be a Group 1er? Absolutely not. Just remember the fact that as a Group 3er, you commonly drop your guard and increase your risk of being victimized. Opportunity (or OBC) breeds criminals like standing water breeds mosquitoes. Most criminals don’t plan to be criminals but when the opportunity presents itself, it’s hard for them to resist. Which brings us to our next chapter, types of criminals.

#PY Tip: Get out of your bubble. Oh, the bubble. What a glorious place to live. The sun is always shining, the temperature is always seventy-two degrees and crime is nonexistent. The bubble is a great place to live until one is victimized. Then, like a figurative blow to the head, it's like the sky is falling. "How could this happen?" "Stuff like this doesn't happen here!" Yeah, we've all heard these people. And they flock to the news camera to profess how little and quiet the town is. Gimme a break, folks!

Wherever there are people, there is crime. Wherever there are human beings, there are victims of crime. That's the truth. However far you bury your head in the sand, it will never be deep enough to escape the phenomenon of people taking advantage of other people. So, now that we've got that straight, let's discuss *bubble towns*.

Bubble towns are where the smallest criminal activity creates the most havoc. A couple smashed car windows in a city barely warrants a police report. However, the same windows smashed in a bubble town constitute front-page news. What's worse than bubble towns are those who live in densely populated areas who think they live in a bubble town. My entire career has been in a bubble town. Eighty percent of the town's boarders are surrounded by a major metropolitan city but listening to some of the residents you'd think there was a medieval moat around it. I've been forced to listen to some of these bubble town reactions: "I can't believe this happened here"; "I thought this was a safe neighborhood!" The best is when they blame the police: "Where were the police when this was going on?" "You should have been patrolling the neighborhood!" Good grief!

The tip is this: Get out of your bubble. Pull your head out of the sand and come to grips with reality: Crime happens where people are!

CHAPTER FIVE
TYPES OF CRIMINALS

There are thousands of people with varying attitudes and behaviors; there are just as many different types of criminals. These criminals are motivated by different desires, influences and experiences. However, because I'm a simpleton, I have broken criminals into four simplistic types. These types are classified based upon the subject's motivation. As with anything in life, people conduct themselves for a purpose. Their behavior is goal oriented. If you're playing soccer, you kick the ball to score a goal.

Millions of Americans wake up at the crack of dawn, travel to work and home and repeat. These people may be motivated by necessity: money to support their families or keep the creditors off their backs. Some work for no other reason than love of the job, while others are motivated by a desire to please others. The vast majority of Americans find that living a legitimate lifestyle, conforming to the laws of the land and providing for those whom they love are all the motivation they need. A great and wise man once told me, “The secret to life is finding what you love to do and figuring out how to make money at it!”

Some Americans seem to embody these principles but are constantly motivated to quench a thirst only criminality can fulfil. Several years ago, I answered a shoplifting call at a high-end women's clothing store. The clerk observed a woman place several items in her purse. The woman continued to look around before leaving the store. Another officer and I greeted her as she attempted to leave. As we interviewed her, she took out her wallet and showed us several credit cards and hundreds of dollars in cash. She said she has plenty of money, but she shoplifted for the thrill. On her criminal record, she had several previous charges for shoplifting, among other larceny crimes. This incident was a new experience for me. Of all the shoplifting arrests I made during my career, I’ve never had someone who was trying to quench a criminal thirst. We were able to recover the stolen goods and charge the woman with shoplifting. Hopefully, she got the mental health treatment she needed.

Unfortunately, there are others (as you'll see here) who are motivated by the desire to hurt others.

The following well-defined categories outline the most common perpetrators who victimize the average American. The four types of criminals are: *petty thieves* motivated by money; *twisted desire*, those motivated by some sort of twisted internal desire; the *mentally challenged*; and the *pure evil.*

Petty Thieves

Petty thieves are just that: petty. However, don't let the name fool you. These criminals are everything from white-collar money launderers to the loser who steals the tip jar at 7-Eleven. Petty thieves are motivated by the goal of obtaining money without earning it. Often it takes just as much work and creativity to complete the crime as it would have done to work at a legitimate job. What's ironic is that if these thieves applied themselves to a lawful business, they'd be rich!

Several years ago, I got a call in the middle of the night for an alarm at a local bank. Bank alarms are the nuisance of all police departments for their overreaction to the slightest breeze. Our function consists of checking the front door, back door and windows. Well, that's exactly what we did and the building looked secure to us. Little did we know, two scumbags were in the building alleviating the bank of as much money as they could get their hands on (most from the ATM).

The following day the sun came up. The manager opened for the morning and found the place cleaned out. He looked at the front door: nothing. He looked at the back door: nothing. Then he found a four-foot hole in the wall of the teller's station. Poking his head through the wall, he found the florist next door.

So, what happened? The petty thieves climbed onto the roof, cut a hole in the ceiling of the florist and then cut another hole in the wall that connected the two stores. Alarm goes off, cops check perimeter and the thieves get away...brilliant! Now, just think if these criminals had applied this knowledge, skill and fortitude to something legitimate!

As the average American citizen, you are most likely to become a victim of this type of criminal. Petty thieves do not like confrontation and try to avoid it at all costs. They want to stay hidden in the shadows. They want to be long gone by the time you realize you've become a victim. One mustn't fear violence from a petty thief; however, be cognizant of their existence. We must coexist with petty thieves, for they walk amongst us disguised as common Americans.

Twisted Desire

A smaller group of individuals can be classified as those motivated by their twisted desire. At some point during these people's lives, their brains had been twisted by an experience, influence or situation. For example, these criminals experienced a traumatic event early in their lives that altered their thought process. More common than not, it's a sexual abuse situation at a young age committed by a trusted family member or authority figure. However, it may also be the result of the influence of a radical theology they've been taught. Either way, what could have been a productive and normal life was perverted somewhere along the way.

To better illustrate this criminal, let's compare them to a computer. If you take that computer to a vacant parking lot and beat the bag out of it with a baseball bat, chances are it's not going to function normally. No matter what you do from that point on, that computer is never going to operate the way it once did. The same goes with the brain of a *twisted desire* criminal. The human brain is a delicate organ that must be coddled and nurtured during those first tender years. Most states have laws protecting the young; these are commonly referred to as the "Tender Years Doctrine." I'm not making any attempt to conjure excuses for this type of person, but it's important to provide an explanation for their acting on pure impulse. These impulses are commonly mistaken for mental illnesses and are often categorized as such by the mental health industry. However, for the purposes of our discussion, it is not a mental illness but an uncontrolled reaction to a situation the criminal may or may not be able to control.

Examples of twisted desire persons are radicalized terrorists, sexual deviants and molesters (no matter their preference). Many are consumed by ideas and ideologies they act out. Even though you're least likely to be victimized by these losers, twisted desire criminals are the most feared. If you watch the evening news on a regular basis, you would think there's an ongoing epidemic of perverts. The impression the media gives us is that if you leave your home, you will be attacked by one of these deviants. However, that's simply not true. The twisted desire criminals lurking in the bushes are few in comparison to the total population. However, that doesn't mean you shouldn't take the necessary steps to protect yourself against them. You owe it to yourself to take the necessary steps to ensure you're not going to be their next victim!

As I write this, there is a national story of a fourteen-year-old girl in Maryland who was raped in the bathroom by two classmates. These classmates were significantly older than her (seventeen and eighteen) and were supposedly illegal immigrants. Whether that is true is inconsequential. What I do know is that these clowns are the very definition of twisted desire. These perverts were interested in quenching their immediate sexual needs at the girl's expense. What's worse is the fact that the finger pointing has already begun. Anti-immigration pundits are exploiting it to their advantage while liberals are remaining silent for more information. Either way, this incident was avoidable. If this crime happened by way of the media explanation, I am confident in making this assertion. As the #PY student, you will learn in the following chapters that you can fight and you can win!

Mentally Challenged

I have included this type of person in this list only due to the frequency of calls we receive about such individuals. Every day, local police departments across the country are inundated with calls about people acting "strangely" or "weird." It has been my experience that in some cases a mentally challenged person acting strangely would, in fact, be committing some sort of crime, whether trespassing, shoplifting or some other petty violation. However, once the police officer responding to the scene makes his assessment, the mental health of the individual far outweighs the minor violation. As recently as the last couple of years, police departments have made significant strides in training street cops how to approach and respond sensitively to this population.

History has taught us that previous responses to these types of calls were flawed. As early as ten to twenty years ago, police officers would respond to a person (who was mentally challenged) acting strangely. Upon the officers' approach, the person would not listen to instructions or directions. The cops, not knowing the person's mental handicap, would perceive this as a threat or breach of peace or law and act accordingly. Through no fault of his own, the police officer would react as trained, arrest the mentally challenged person and charge him criminally. Often the charges would consist of disorderly conduct, failure to comply or some other minor misdemeanor. The case would subsequently be dismissed after the district attorney or judge learned that the person was mentally challenged or simply due to the fact that the crime was so minor. However, the damage was done. There was no connection between the responding officer and the mentally challenged person. The person now views the police officer as an advisory and will never trust the police in the future.

With recent training being offered by many departments around the country, police officers have tools to help them identify an individual who is mentally challenged or possibly experiencing a life crisis. They can alter their approach and establish a bond. As a result, this person is led to professional, psychological help and avoids the criminal justice system. Does this mean you don't need to protect yourself from them? Absolutely not! Mentally challenged people are just as unpredictable and dangerous as anybody else – in some cases, I'd venture to say even more so. When they become scared in an unknown environment or situation, they may react violently and hurt those around him. Your job as a #PY student is to be able to recognize this behavior and then steer clear of it.

Pure Evil

It's unfortunate that these people exist. Pure evil people are interested only in causing pain to another. Like the twisted desire population, their brains may have been manipulated by a negative experience, influence or situation. Pure evil criminals are commonly referred to as "animals," but I find the connection inappropriate. Animals' only motivation is survival. They kill other animals to eat and endure the wild. Evil people, on the other hand, are motivated by the desire to create havoc and ruin lives. They enjoy the thrill they get by killing, destroying and causing pain. I like the analogy of a virus. Viruses feed off healthy cells and cause nothing but sickness and death. That is their function.

I can offer no explanation as to why these people exist. My only comfort is the world can't have the very good without the very bad. Pure evil criminals walk among us every day and they're not going away. Often, they hide in plain sight – the guy in line in front of you at the restaurant and the guy standing in front of the convenience store in your neighborhood. You may erroneously believe you reside in a good neighborhood or expensive town, and that this type of criminal can't get to you. Unfortunately, that's not even remotely true. Browsing your state's online sex offender database will open your eyes. These people live in your state, town and neighborhood.

What's more, many who may not reside next door are passing through your community as transients or gypsies. Many of them move from town to town doing laborious trade work like construction and get paid in cash. These transients visit your neighborhood and prey on the weak, vulnerable or individuals who otherwise have faith in mankind. Hell, this guy could be cleaning your neighbor's pool right now! They do quality work, they get paid and they're gone the next day. Hopefully, during their brief stay in your "safe" neighborhood, they don't get tempted by the neighbor or the early morning jogger.

In 2001 Gary Lee Sampson traveled up and down Route 95 killing people. Sampson was a truck driver who was wanted for bank robbery in North Carolina. His victims included three men: two in Massachusetts (his home state) and one in New Hampshire. The fourth victim, in Vermont, survived a similar attack by Sampson. Even though these incidents occurred within the short span of a week, people in these states learned no lessons. After Sampson was caught, everybody breathed a proverbial sigh of relief. They collectively thought that since Sampson had been apprehended, there was nothing to be afraid of anymore. What's more, the belief that Gary Lee is an anomaly is laughable. With the popularity of social media and online publications, we know more up-to-the-minute information than we did in 2001. The world gets smaller and smaller every day. And, of course, people now have confirmation that Sampson was not the anomaly we thought he was.

Pure evil criminals are evil all the time. The mere fact that they're skimming the pool does not mean their brains are not corrupted by the devil. These are not the people who are otherwise normal and snap one day. No, these are the population you hear about who kill, kidnap and torture other human beings. As a #PY student, you will be prepared to protect yourself against this criminal.

#PY Tip: Be active, not reactive. First order of business: Do you recognize him? If not, don't take your eyes off him. Whether you're walking past him in the hallway or he's approaching your stationary position, your eyes never divert from him. This may be difficult because your mother always told you not to stare, but it may save your life. He's waiting for you to divert your attention so he can get the jump on you; it's as simple as that. By not diverting your eyes, you're ensuring that your reaction time will be faster and more accurate if you see the threat right away. Compare that to keeping your eyes on the floor when his hands come out of his pockets and latch onto your face. No matter the reaction, it won't be good enough! No, as a #PY student, you hold up your hands, defending against his grasp before it reaches your face. Then, in a twisting, shoulder-down motion, you're running like the building is on fire.

CHAPTER SIX
TYPES OF CRIME

There are only two types of crime: property and violent. These are the only ways you'll be victimized by crime. That's it! Not as glamorous or sophisticated as the media or the entertainment world would lead you to believe. Thus, if you mentally prepare to address these two types of crime systematically, you'll be ready to protect yourself under any circumstance. In short, the system you'll need to develop involves prioritizing your *Dominant Defenses*. This system consists of deciding between defending yourself or your property. You must begin by mentally preparing in advance because if you're faced with a situation, you may have only seconds to decide. Just as a police officer is required to make a split-second decision to take lethal action, you must decide on your dominant defense.

The theory of dominant defense begs the question: Who would sacrifice personal safety for their property? I'll respond with an example. Every summer, when forest fires spread in northern California, the media broadcasts video of some poor homeowner spraying his house with a garden hose. He's spraying the exterior of his home with water as the glow of fire looms behind him. Or this: The convenience store owner who fights off an armed robber with a golf club. These two examples are classified under the category of what I call *property-dominant* victimization. Instead of conceding and heading for the hills, these two decided to put their personal safety in jeopardy to protect their property.

The alternative is when the seemingly reasonable person would rather sacrifice their meager possessions to protect themselves. This I identify as *self-dominant* victimization. Of course, one really doesn't know how they'll react until they are put in either of these positions. I'd like to think that if my personal security were being threatened, I would have the wherewithal to turn and screw. However, my ego has played a role in previous life decisions that weren't in my best interest. In the following sections, I'll describe each type of crime as well as subcategories of each.

#PY Exercise: While reading this, ponder which type of person you are: property-dominant or self-dominant. Also, in the examples given, take a second and decide how you would likely react in a similar situation.

Property Crime

Property crime is the most common type of victimization. As I mentioned in previous chapters, petty thieves want to take your stuff without being seen and without you knowing about it. They take your stuff and sell it to a fence. A *fence* is someone who may have a legitimate business but who buys stolen items and sells them retail. For example, there are a number of convenience store owners in the Boston area who "place their orders" with local shoplifters. These shoplifters will visit the local CVS or Walgreens and steal a whole rack of one type of item. I've seen people run out of stores with a jacket full of toothpaste. It's pretty comical. Many assume it's stolen for personal consumption. However, if you've ever caught one of these guys and spoken to them up close, you'd realize the insides of their mouths haven't seen toothpaste in years! When I was new to police work, several of the dinosaurs informed me that the "order" had been placed. If the thief gets away, he returns to the convenience store and gives the owner a jacket full of shampoo. The merchant then stocks his shelves and sells the toothpaste at retail to make a hefty profit. He pays the thief a nominal fee and the cycle continues. If the police ever come knocking at the merchant's door, he claims, "Oh, I don't know where he got it from." Yadda, yadda.

A homeowner's stuff is liquidated using the same process. Anything the thief takes (preferably something that will fit into his pocket, e.g., jewelry, wallet, credit cards, etc.), he finds someone who's willing to pay for it.

Ponder this: When you're at work during the day, how many people visit your front door? Never thought about it? Well, you need to. Between the mailman, the UPS delivery guy, the meter reader, the dry cleaner flyer man and the Jehovah's Witnesses, your front stoop is a pretty busy place. It goes without saying that these stoop dwellers don't get a second look. The old law-enforcement saying is *criminals break into your home from the back at night and the front during the day*. This couldn't be more true. Most breaking-and-entering criminals will first visit the front stoop and ring the bell. If there's no answer, the criminal gives the knob and lock a quick check. Once he's confirmed they're both secure, it becomes a matter of a

Ray Bourque hip check or a backwards donkey kick, forcing the wood to splinter.

Recently, I responded to a breaking-and-entering in-progress call in which the junkie visited the front door and rang the bell. Not expecting any visitors, the victim didn't bother looking out the window. Thus, when nobody came to the door, the thief smashed a six-inch by six-inch decorative window that adorned the door. He reached through the broken glass and unlocked the deadbolt. Once inside, he began his looting spree. Upon hearing the smashing glass, the homeowner ran out the back door and called 9-1-1. Three other units and I were there in seconds. When confronted in the dining room, the criminal dove head first through the dining room window. The officer who witnessed this Jimmy-the-Superfly-Snooker move couldn't believe what he was seeing. The sound of his body slamming into the glass sounded like an explosion. Needless to say, our criminal was busted. He suffered some serious head trauma and was brought to the hospital before court.

The point of this story is that I thought the victim did everything right. She knew someone was in her home and instead of calling out or confronting this loser, she exited the home and called us. Had she called out (like most people would do in the situation), he would've been scared off and long gone before we got there.

However, if she had confronted him while he was in the home, the criminal's fight-or-flight instincts may have kicked in and he could have assaulted her. Still, with that said, there were many things she could have done to make her home less appealing to this junkie.

This seems like a better time than any to note the different names for crimes. Most states have specific names for "charges," but they're all based on the same prohibited conduct. For example, a home is burglarized, not robbed. People – not buildings – are robbed. In Massachusetts, the term for a burglary is *Breaking and Entering* or some variation of this (entering without breaking; B+E day/night time, etc.). This really isn't important beyond the fact that it annoys law enforcement beyond comprehension when they're misused or transposed. This is not to suggest that one type of crime is more or less important than the other; they're both highly emotional experiences. However, when a victim calls the police and tells the dispatcher they were *robbed* when, in fact, their home was *burglarized*, the police response may be somewhat different. For example, when a home is burglarized, there may be a significant delay in reporting. The homeowner comes home from work to find the window smashed and the criminal long gone. However, when one is robbed on the street, the victim has just experienced a violent encounter and the criminal may still be in the area. Thus, the response by police to a burglarized home may be one patrol unit and a detective to process the scene, while the response to a robbery may be six or seven cruisers canvassing the neighborhood.

Back to our story: Upon reflection, I noted several items that made this home appealing to Joe Dirtbag. First, the bushes in the front yard were overgrown to the point that the front door could not be seen from the street. When I do security home evaluations I commonly hear all the excuses: the bushes block noise from the street, the shade keeps the home cool in the summer, yadda yadda. The truth is, this particular home would not have been targeted if Joe Dirtbag could have been seen smashing the front door. He chose this home, on a busy street where pedestrians often walk by, for a reason. My opinion is that he chose this home because he could not be seen past the bushes.

Next, small windows on or around the front door drive me nuts. Modern doors have made significant improvements to their construction to protect them against being smashed. However, at the end of the day, it's only glass. Given enough force, even the toughest glass will smash. In the above case, the front door to our victim's home predated the Kennedy administration and, thus, was an easy target.

Finally, the homeowner took no advantage of modern technology to defend against intruders. For example, alarm systems or surveillance cameras work wonders with regard to creating a deterrence. I know what you're gonna say...she was home, so the alarm wouldn't have been set. I realize that, but some systems employ a chime when an exterior door is opened. What's more, an alarm decal on the window or a visible alarm panel may have been enough to deter our scumbag. The products being made today are getting better and better. There's a system called "Ring" that acts as a doorbell with a camera. When someone rings the bell, the homeowner gets an alert on their smart phone. The homeowner can interact with Joe Dirtbag through the homeowner's cell phone a million miles away. This does two things. One, it gives the impression that you're inside, which may scare away our loser. Two, you can visually observe the dirtbag and record the interaction in the event he does break in. Security alarm companies are making it easier for the general public to affordably protect themselves.

My Home is My Castle

My wife thinks I'm crazy. Since my son was born, I've gone above and beyond when it comes to securing our home. My previous attitude was *let them break in, my Smith and*

Wesson would love to meet them. That was fine when it was just me, but my family also needs tools to safeguard the home when I'm not around. Recently, I was on an Executive Protection detail that brought me to the western border of Massachusetts. Even though I was far away, I was reassured that my family was safe because I had taken the extra steps and implemented the proper tools. Some of these tools are explained below in the *#PY Tips* section of this chapter. Even though some of them may be considered prehistoric, they're highly effective.

Most states have adopted a reasonable approach toward helping people protect themselves inside their homes. For states that have not, courts have recognized the common-law definition of the Castle Law. The *Castle Law* (or Castle Doctrine) suggests that if one unlawfully enters your home, you can reasonably defend yourself. Of course, luring someone into your home is indefensible, but if someone kicks in your door and corners you, you would be protected. Other states haven't adopted the Castle Doctrine and suggest that occupants have a duty to retreat to avoid a violent attack. They seem to say that even though you're in your home, minding your own business, it's YOUR duty to leave. Believe that? To this I say: No way! If some clown is breaking into my home in the middle of the night, why does the responsibility fall on me to run into the street in my pajamas? (That is, if I'm wearing pajamas.) That recommendation is unreasonable. With that said, even though the law is on the books in these states, I can't fathom any municipal police department turning the screws on a resident for defending his family in his home. Still, stranger things have happened.

#PY Tip 1: Dowel Stoppage: One of the best ways to prevent break-ins is also the simplest. One needs only a one-inch dowel and a saw (and maybe a Home Depot in the area). What you're going to do is place the dowel in the track of your sliding door or double-hung window. If placed correctly, the dowel will prevent the door or window from opening. I know what the firefighters are going to say: "What if there's a fire in the home? How are we gonna get in?" Well, I think that's what Halligans are for. For those who don't know, a Halligan is a tool firefighters use to smash things. Thus, if the only escape method is through the window, I'm confident the occupants will have the wherewithal to remove the stick of wood and slide it open. Otherwise, take a chair and make shards out of that window!

Unfortunately, this technique does not work with crank-out casement windows. However, dowels in a double-hung window track are like kryptonite. I cut the dowel about an inch or two shorter than necessary for easy set-up and removal. I've seen some that have handles or knobs screwed into to them for lifting out – creative but perhaps unnecessary.

As you can see in the above image, a one inch dowel is in the track of the sliding door.

One thing you can't depend on is window locks between the top and bottom portions of the double-hung window. These are so easily defeated, it's crazy. However, deploying both tools almost guarantees a source of frustration for the criminal to the point that he'll give up and try your neighbor's house!

#PY Tip 2: Deadbolt: For the love of God, install deadbolts on all your doors. It's so simple that not deploying them borders on the insane. Similar to vulnerable window locks, the pin-and-tumbler locks on doorknobs are very easily defeated. What's even more astounding is the licensing requirements – or lack thereof – for locksmiths. Some states have no licensing, bonding or oversight of the locksmithing profession. Believe that? Anybody can buy lock-picking tools – more specifically, a manual lock pick gun – for less than twenty bucks. A lock pick gun is a tool in which a rod is inserted into a keyhole and, when the trigger is pulled, it unlocks the door. The rod smacks the pins a couple times so that they retract into the top of the tumbler, thereby releasing the spindle. Technical stuff, right? Buy one of these on eBay and you have access to about ninety percent of homes in the United States.

However, as a #PY student you've got the upper hand. Before snuggling into bed, you deployed a sophisticated deadbolt guaranteed to frustrate any criminal. Remember, none of these techniques is foolproof. They're intended to frustrate and challenge the criminal enough that he either can't get in or makes enough noise to attract your attention.

#PY Tip 3: Who's Home?: One of my favorite crime prevention tools is a product called *Fake TV*. This product was advertised on television a decade ago and can still be found on the internet. Using a timer, it emits a blue light to give the impression that a television is on inside the home. The blue light flickers and moves just as a real television would. As long as the shades are drawn, nobody can tell the difference.

Not long ago, I had a client who owns a seasonal home on Cape Cod. During the off season, he deployed the Fake TV in his living room. One year, his neighborhood suffered from a rash of residential break-ins, with thieves stealing televisions, stereos, computers, even silver flatware. This client said he didn't know whether it was the Fake TV or some other mitigating factor, but almost every home in his neighborhood got burglarized except his. Visit YouTube and search for "Fake TV." Watch a video of it working and decide for yourself whether it serves as a deterrent. For twenty bucks, how can you go wrong?!

#PY Tip 4: Timed Lights: Along the same lines as a Fake TV, lamps on timers can deter home break-ins. Lights going on and off during the night will confuse and disorient a potential burglar. Picture this: Two homes are side by side. Both have the same amount of yard lighting and no cars in the driveway. The one on the left has a television flickering in the upstairs window, while a lamp just turned on in the living room. The one on the right is in complete darkness. Which one would you think is occupied? The one on the right is clearly the optimal target for our scumbag.

#PY Tip 5: Bathroom Door: This technique was introduced to me by my wife. I learned this the hard way when I came home one day while she was showering. Unfortunately, nature was calling and I ran upstairs from the driveway only to find that she had locked the bathroom door. When the dust settled (and after I had made other arrangements), I asked her why she had locked the bathroom door when she was home alone. She said, “In case of a burglary, they’re not getting in here to surprise me. If they started to break down the door, I’d hear them!” What genius. Just another level of protection when home alone and most vulnerable.

#PY Tip 6: Snow Tracks: Sometimes we can use our environment to protect ourselves. When I conduct residential security patrols, I always make a point to drive up and down the driveway several times. Most of these patrols are for residents on vacation, so they don’t mind my headlights in and out of their yard. Several sets of tire tracks in the snow give no conformational indication that the residents are home. One set of tracks from the garage to the street indicates nobody’s home. But what if the car pulled out of the garage, onto the street and then back into the driveway. If they did this several times, nobody could determine whether the owner was home. Similar to the lamp timers and Fake TV, this is a technique to confuse and disorient the scumbag!

#PY Tip 7: Keypad for Quick Entry: When I conduct security surveys, I recommend that homeowners choose one door on which to install a digital keypad lock. This is primarily for convenience, but it has a security component as well. If you ever find yourself locked out of the home (or being chased by a pack of rabid dogs), you don't have to fumble with keys. As a police officer, I consistently respond to calls in which the resident has locked themselves out of their home. I know...it's hard to believe people call the police for this, but we get several a month. Personally, I would call a locksmith, but that's just me. Nonetheless, the fire department arrives and deploys a tall ladder to get into a window or back porch. This embarrassing situation can be avoided with a hundred-dollar keyless entry system.

#PY Tip 8: Never "Check In" on Facebook: Ugh...I don't know where to begin with this one. I can't comprehend why anybody would advertise the fact that they're away from home. This is exactly what they're doing: advertising. What's worse is the fact that those who are "checking in" are the same people who "friend" acquaintances or people they don't know. As a private investigator, I have access to private data source information not obtainable by the public. However, I often have more luck with public records then with paid databases. These include court records, real estate transactions, even the white pages to discover where people live. Now apply this information to the information posted on Facebook and voila…all the flatware silver and laptops I can fence!

Larceny

Department Store Zombie: People tend to drop their guard in supermarkets and department stores. I'm not sure why that is other than that their minds are so focused on the application of material things, they're not *radius aware*. This is the ideal situation for Joe Scumbag to get his filthy hand in your purse and swipe your wallet. Of course, you don't realize you've been victimized until checkout. Meanwhile, "Joe" is on his way to the liquor store to charge your credit card. My mother had her wallet stolen several years ago and a couple hundred dollars was charged to her card at a supermarket. Her attitude was, "Well, at least I fed someone for the week!" My cynical brain said, "C'mon, Mom, they also sell liquor, cigarettes and lottery tickets at the supermarket!"

Thus, I've included the following tips to prevent this from happening to you. As stated before, many are common sense, but still need restating.

#PY Tip 1: What's Expendable?: I've noticed that women carry the kitchen sink with them. I call my wife's purse *the satchel*. Being a mom, she has everything from makeup to hand sanitizer to receipts from two years ago. When pushing a shopping carriage, many moms keep their satchels in the baby section of the shopping cart. The rationale is "I'm right here, nobody's gonna bother it." However, it takes only a pair of slacks or new lip gloss to distract your attention long enough for Johnny Scumbag to relieve you of your wallet. During investigations, I've seen it via surveillance footage. In the town where I work, most businesses have cameras and NASA-quality, high-tech playback systems. When I respond to these calls, I make contact with the loss prevention representative to view the footage. I'm able to watch Johnny Scumbag slip his hand into a purse and within a millisecond, the wallet is gone. Thus, the lesson here is to take your wallet out of your purse and put it in your jacket pocket. If you can't leave your purse in your car (or at home), consider its contents expendable. Of course, when I say leave it in your car, I mean secure it in the trunk or some other place that is "out of plain sight." This includes under the seat, in the glove compartment or under the storage cover screen of your SUV. Don't tempt Johnny Scumbag while he's strolling through the parking lot.

This goes for men as well. Many of us carry our wallets in the back pockets of our strong hand. When in crowded places (train stations, hockey games, etc.), put your wallet in your FRONT pocket and make consistent checks. Pickpockets look for wallets in back pockets, bump into an unsuspecting victim and like that – wallet gone!

#PY Tip 2: Protect Your Radius: People drop their guard in stores and supermarkets because their brains are linear: They can focus on only one task at a time. Well, the #PY student must be bilinear. Yes, focus on the green beans or the ingredients in tonight's taco salad, but not at the expense of your radius. The aisles in a supermarket in my town are so small, two carts barely make it past one another. It's not uncommon for people to bump into each other during high-traffic Saturdays or weeknights just before dinnertime. These are the ideal times for the *ol' pickpocket dash*. What's funny is that Johnny Scumbag looks like the average neighbor. The reaction most people have when they bump into someone is to turn toward the person and excuse himself. The person who did the bumping raises no red flags because of his non-threatening appearance. The lesson here is to check anyway. Take a swipe of your pocket and make sure your wallet is still there...just in case. Make a quick tap of your jacket or pants pocket and continue your shopping.

#PY Tip 3: The Grinch is Real: We read about these stories every holiday season. People shop at malls and other shopping plazas and hit several stores. Shoppers don't want to carry several bags of recently purchased gifts from store to store, so what do they do? They stop off at the car and drop them off. Good idea, right? The #PY student knows that this is a terrible idea. Johnny Scumbag will surveil the parking lot from a parked car. Because stores know that marketing never ends, they print the company logo on the shopping bag for you to carry to your car. Now, Johnny Scumbag may not know the contents of the bag, but he knows where it came from. He may direct his attention to victims carrying Best Buy or jewelry store bags. He follows the victim to the trunk of her vehicle. Once she heads back to the store for more shopping, he makes his move. He saves time by knowing exactly where she stored the items, making a quick hit and a quick score.

Unfortunately, this #PY tip requires a little more effort for the #PY student. You need to either carry all your bags or make shorter mall trips. This is blasphemy to those midnight Black Friday shoppers, but it's a gamble I'm not willing to take.

Car Breaks

Perhaps the most common type of property crime is when one's car gets broken into. Most people assume that the crook smashes the window and steals the contents. However, it's been my experience that most people become victims because of the simple fact that they don't lock their car doors. What else can I say?

Graffiti

If you're a property owner in an urban setting, one of the ways you may be victimized is through graffiti. Graffiti is one of the lowest forms of so-called "art." Many "taggers" would be considered very talented if they employed another medium on which to display their work. However, these criminals decide to commit a crime by defacing your property.

Every year when summer rears its delightful head, I'm reminded of school vacations I had growing up. Trips to the community pool, games of stickball in the park and cookouts with family. Ah, how simple life was back then. But I'm also reminded of those summer breakers who have nothing better to do than cause mischief and headaches for the "elders." Just to be clear, I was not one of these juveniles (no matter what my mom says!).

Some of these mischief makers express their artistic side by spray painting walls and fences with nonsense. These mini van Gogh's cause hundreds, or even thousands, of dollars of damage with each canvass. So, as a property owner, how do you protect yourself? There are two proven ways to accomplish this. First, hire a uniformed security company to conduct random physical security patrols that detect and deter trespassers. This is popular for many commercial buildings that are unoccupied off hours. For a flat daily rate, security officers will patrol property on foot or in a vehicle, find trouble-seeking youth and advise them that they need to relocate themselves. Most young trespassers avoid trouble and just need to be reminded that your property is not a hangout!

The second way to prevent trespassers is to install motion-activated lighting around your property. These don't have to be ultra-expensive and you don’t need an electrician to install them. Affordable units can be found at your local hardware store and installed in any incandescent light bulb socket. Once the trespassers cross the path, the light will illuminate and hopefully scare them off. Other lights illuminate when the sun goes down and it gets dark. Most "taggers" require the cover of darkness to commit their crime, so take away that element!

Cybercrime

Computer-based crime or *cybercrime* is a specialized type of property crime. With the advent and convenience of technology, the threat is getting worse by the day. The more lackadaisical we as Americans become with online shopping and banking, the more opportunity criminals have to target us. In fact, if I were entering college now, I'd seriously consider computer-based crime as my major.

One of the most common ways criminals prey on victims is phishing. I recently received an email from a credit card company with which I do business. I read the email twice and thought, *Would my credit card company really attempt to contact me using email? I don't think so*. Being the suspicious, skeptical person I am, I called the credit card company using the phone number printed on the back of my card. Lo and behold, my credit card company doesn't even have my email address on file. Imagine that. What's more, the service representative said it happens so frequently, the company doesn't investigate these claims anymore.

••••○ AT&T LTE 11:11 AM

< Inbox (2)

Chase Online
To: Undisclosed recipien... more...

CO

Urgent: Security Alert On Your Account
Today at 10:42 AM

CHASE®

Dear Customer

Chase Online recently closed one of your accounts due to inactivity and suspicious login attempt. To reopen the closed account immediately follow the update account link below.

Click on https://www.chase.com/verif y/mlogin to complete verification process.

This link will expire in 24 hour, so be sure to use it right away. Failure to verify your details will make you vulnerable and exposed to hacking threats and losing your account online access.

Thank you for choosing Chase.

Sincerely,

Chese Online.

In my case, the email looked unbelievably accurate. The company logo adorned the top of the message and the email address started with "service" and ended with the company name *dot com*. One thing that immediately drew my attention was the way in which several sentences in the email were phrased. Everything was spelled correctly but when I read the sentence out loud, it didn't sound quite right. I later learned that the reason for this was that the email did not originate in the U.S. and English was the author's second language. Thus, the author did not phrase the email as an American would. In addition, the email asked me to click a specific attached link to log into my account. That didn't sound right, either. In the end, I wasn't fooled and neither should you be. Here are a couple of helpful hints courtesy of the National Association of Federal Credit Unions:

#PY Tip 1: Never respond to an unsolicited email that asks for detailed financial information. In my case, I didn’t click on the link. If I had, it most likely would've sent me to a website that would have required my username, password, account number, date of birth or other identifying information. I've heard of incidents in which clicking the link took the person to a site and asked for just a username and password. When this information was entered, the next screen read something like, "I'm sorry but our system is down, try again later." The victim went about their day not knowing that their username and password had been recorded and account was being cleaned out.

#PY Tip 2: Report anything suspicious to the proper authorities. If you believe you were scammed, or if your account has been hacked, always report it to your local police department. As long as there is a monetary loss, or potential for loss, your local police department is obligated to document the information and conduct an investigation. Most local departments are involved with state law enforcement agencies that track this type of cybercrime. Even though many phishing scams are conducted across country lines, financial institutions are prepared to assist you only AFTER you've reported it to a law enforcement agency. In addition to notifying law enforcement, you should put a fraud alert on your credit report by contacting all the major credit bureaus: Equifax, Experian and Trans Union. Also, contact the Internet Crime Complaint Center; this agency is a partnership between the FBI and the National White Collar Crime Center and can be reached at www.ic3.gov.

Civil Crime

In the second chapter I mentioned that there are only two types of crime: *property* and *violent*. However, civil victimizations can be just as emotional and distressing as criminal victimization. Civil issues can include situations in which you've made a business deal that went sour or a domestic partnership that unceremoniously ended.

#PY Tip 1: Hire a PI: One of the ways to protect yourself is by obtaining information. There are many sources of information if you know where to look. Often, when we're dealing with a new and unknown situation, information seems unobtainable. The private investigation industry is a profession devoted solely to gathering and analyzing information. That information may be in the form of data, statistical information, surveillance observations or various types of witness statements. As a licensed private investigator, I receive daily calls from prospective clients who require investigation of various civil situations. It's always interesting to hear some of the questions people have about what information I can and can't find. As always, I'm as truthful as possible and explain why I may or may not be able to find information. Sometimes there's an awkward pause on the phone as I'm staring off into space, thinking about their question or the type of investigation. I explain to them that I'm contemplating my investigative approach or what information I'd need to obtain.

This begs the question: How does a prospective client determine whether I'm the private investigator to hire? Is it just that I'm willing to make the effort and listen? Or is there something more? Hiring a PI is not as easy as one might think. Consider this: If you were hiring a contractor or painter, the first thing you'd expect to see are examples of recent work. If you were hiring a nanny or daycare, you'd ask for references. Unfortunately, the PI business is very protective of our clients' information, and our classified information is just that: classified! Thus, the following #PY tips will help those who may be looking to hire a private detective.

#PY Tip 2: License: This one is obvious, but the first thing you need to look for is licensing. The private detective business is highly scrutinized. For example, the licensing agency in Massachusetts is the state police, which conducts a thorough background check. There is nothing cops hate more than people pretending to be cops. Licensing agencies have very strict applicant requirements. In addition, once one is licensed, there is a litany of procedures one must follow or their license may be in jeopardy. Very good records are kept of complaints and/or subsequent suspensions or non-renewals. Most licensed PI's welcome this kind of scrutiny because it keeps investigators honest and prevents wannabe PI's from taking advantage of someone who needs help. If there is even a question about a detective license status, call the local licensing division in your area.

#PY Tip 3: Initial Conversation: One thing that irritates me to no end (and this goes for any profession) is someone who takes work they're not qualified for. We call this *Starving Artist Syndrome*; they need the work so badly, they say yes to anything. During the initial conversation, make note of whether the investigator "yeses" you to death. Are you asking them to do something that may be inappropriate or even criminal and their response is “Oh, yeah, we can do that.” One thing to pay attention to is whether they’re asking you questions. The investigator is supposed to be a professional detective, so if he asks no follow-up questions, a red flag should go up. I can’t tell you how many times I've been asked to locate someone and, after asking my series of questions (including their relationship with the person, any restraining orders, and of course WHY they want to find this person), I’ve told the potential client, “Sorry, that's not something I can do.” Then there are the people who lie to me: “I don't know if she has a restraining order against me...” Sorry, buddy! So, you need to look elsewhere if the investigator's only response to your inquiry is “Yes, yes, yes...what's your credit card number?”

#PY Tip 4: Specialization: Does this investigator or company specialize in the type of investigation you're requesting? Several years ago, the PI landscape was filled with so-called *generalists* who would conduct any type of investigation under the sun. One day they’re following a cheating spouse and the next they're conducting a corporate investigation of an employee stealing company funds. Even though many of these agencies still exist (and are very competent), private detectives today are specializing in unique types of investigations. Several of my colleagues conduct only cheating spouse and domestic investigations, and make a very good living. Even though I have a lot of experience in this type of investigation, it's not my specialty. My humble opinion is that a specialist conducts a certain type of investigation day-in and day-out. Her brain is constantly trained on its approach, sequence or conclusion, and that experience is invaluable.

Civil Disorder/Riotous Behavior

It's a very frustrating time to be an American. In the 240 years of our nation's existence, we've never been more divided. Not since the 13th amendment have individual member citizens fought so hard against each other. The country is separated. We can blame all the politicians or just those who disagree with us, but there is a much simpler explanation.

In the old days, if you wanted current information, you were limited by a handful of television networks or newspaper outlets. Books did not provide current news simply because they couldn't be printed fast enough. Thus, we had to rely on the newscaster to provide that information. Most times, they did a fine job at being fair, balanced and unbiased. For the most part, they presented information from both sides of the argument. This forced the viewer to listen to opposing views and find the viewpoint they agreed with. Sometimes the viewer found themselves nodding to those opposing viewpoints and saying, “Yeah, I see your point.”

Today, however, with the advent of up-to-the-second digital media (namely, social media), we can pick and choose the information we care to receive. For example, on Facebook and Instagram I follow only “news” media that are pro-police or that don’t disparage my profession. I choose only the information I want to hear. Those with similar opinions can’t stomach anything that defames a fellow police officer. Is that fair? Of course not. I know police officers are flawed and imperfect. I’m aware that some of us use their badge/position to take advantage of others. Even though I get that, the fact is, I don’t want to hear about it! I’ve simply removed opposing viewpoints from the conversation in my head.

Due to the fact that we now have access to thousands (and, dare I say, millions) of “news providers,” many of us target only those who share our opinions. So, the lefties will listen only to lefties and the righties will listen only to the righties. God forbid, somehow one of the opposing opinions enters our scrolling feed…"triggered!"

This theory would explain the explosion of "demonstrations" in the last couple of years. We've learned that people will protest anything, anywhere, for any reason. The other day there was a nationwide organized demonstration with a message to the President of the United States to release his tax returns. Whether or not you agree with the individual, the election is over, so why resurrect this discussion? The simple explanation is that the demonstrators needed something to demonstrate. They needed something to justify their existence. Nothing illustrated this more than when information leaked about why the Occupy Wall Street movement organized. It appears a Canadian group, *Adbusters*, took a poll on its website and social media asking the masses what they should protest next. The reply: big business!

Whether the disdain is for a person (politician) or a system (government), people will act out their frustrations. As long as there's a system of norms, rules or governance, there will be people who "rebel" against it. During these outward shows of rebellious actions, law enforcement is taught to target the leaders should they become unruly. Most big-city law enforcement agencies have units dedicated to identifying "radical" groups and exploiting their recruitment efforts.

These specialty units locate and identify leaders on social media with the intent to disrupt their next demonstration.

The theory is that if the "leader" is taken out of the picture, the sheep can't be herded. Historically, the most difficult thing about this is identifying the so-called leader. However, with the popularity of social media as a recruitment tool, identifying the leader has become a fairly simple task. The "leaders" of the radical groups are not shy in their social media posts with regard to their messages and day-to-day operations. However, these masterminds shut off their YouTube cameras when Mom comes down to the basement with their sandwiches with the crusts cut off. They remain charismatic enough to get others to follow them, and follow they do.

Many of these groups give the impression that they're part of a larger organization and endorsed internationally. However, many are lone wolf operations that seek the support of more mainstream organizations. Thus, by default, local demonstrations become the work of larger groups.

How do we – as normal, everyday Americans – protect ourselves from these losers? The first defense is knowledge. Type the names of these groups with your hometown into a Google search and see what comes up. For example, this morning I Googled “Antifa Boston” and found this group's Facebook page. I’m welcomed to the website by a woman wearing a handkerchief across her face and her fist in the air. She offers an overview of this local chapter, including how the “alt-right” are Nazi fascists who have the support of the state and police. She goes on to say that she’s forced to cover her face with a handkerchief to avoid becoming a victim of police authoritarianism. Give me a break, folks!

Anyway, what they’ve conveniently included on their Facebook pages is a list of upcoming events. These include *Boston People’s Climate Mobilization* on Saturday and a *May Day Rally for Workers and Immigrants* on Monday. As you know, Facebook allows users to express interest in events. What I find hilarious is that Saturday’s event has just under 5,000 people expressing interest, but only 400 are interested in Monday’s event. Apparently, Monday’s event isn’t important enough to skip first period.

#PY Tip: Periodically visit these websites and check out their upcoming events. If you work or live in the area of an upcoming “demonstration,” try to avoid it. The last thing you need is to be stuck in traffic during a resistance movement. Even worse is suffering injury or having your car damaged while just passing through.

Remember, these people have nothing to lose and will do anything to express their message.

On January 15, 2015 at 7:30 a.m., six people inserted their arms into barrels that were deposited onto Boston's Route 93 and chained themselves together. For those who don't know, Route 93 is one of the heaviest-traveled roads – if not the heaviest-traveled road – in and out of Boston. As a result of this *activism*, the highway was shut down for several hours, creating a disaster of a morning commute. In addition, ambulances had to be rerouted around the demonstration and diverted to hospitals at which they hadn't intended to stop. Thankfully, the delay resulted in no deaths, but the possibility of a delayed hospital response put many in a dangerous situation. Of course, this type of demonstration was unforeseen and unavoidable. However, it illustrates a complete lack of compassion for anybody else but their "message." This message, by the way, was completely diluted in this ridiculous venture. In fact, ask most Bostonians about this event and they can't even recall what the message was. In the following weeks, several news outlets tracked down these douche barrels. One loser was interviewed on the porch of his parents' million-dollar home in a wealthy neighborhood and offered his ridiculous explanation. C'mon, man!

Commercial Property

Owning a business is like living a second life. A business is a living, breathing organism. It has the same basic requirements as a person. It must be fed, harbored, encouraged and secured. When leaving for the night, the owner must ensure that it's protected from victimization. Whether the criminal's goal is to obtain merchandise or information, or even just temporary shelter, the owner must protect against it.

#PY Tip 1: If the business is located in a strip mall, consistently talk to the other business owners in that location. When I was a mall security guard, I learned of a mutual aid organization between several of the other stores that met on a semi-monthly basis. What they would commonly discover is that they were being targeted by the same shoplifters. In addition, several had been the victims of attempted break-ins at night. This shared information proved that their victimization was not isolated. They eventually teamed up and put significant pressure on the landlord for stricter security advancements.

In the town where I work as a police officer, several banks have teamed up to share information about suspicious persons. They'll share photos and conversations that tellers had with these "customers," keeping each other informed. This keeps bank employees on the lookout for strange behavior and encourages them to take note when they encounter such people. It goes without saying that bank robbers are not a sophisticated bunch. Often, before they strike, robbers visit several banks in a specific geographical area, looking for the weak link: the bank where tellers or security personnel aren't paying attention. This may take two or three visits. They'll pretend to be customers, ask strange questions. Once they find their "weak link," they'll strike or move on to the next one. With this shared information, the banks have taken a proactive first step toward protecting themselves.

#PY Tip 2: Window to Victimization: I'm amazed at how many convenience stores get robbed. It's hard to believe that with the advent of digital pay, credit cards and debit cards, robbing a convenience store remains profitable. However, it happens every day. What's even more astounding is that many stores have taken no proactive steps to protect themselves. Until recently, the town where I work had convenience stores on every corner. They all sold the same stuff, but each one was more convenient than the last one. As I patrolled my route, I would glance into each window to ensure the clerk was okay. Often, I would get frustrated that the owner (in all his wisdom) had posted posters or advertisements that blocked the view inside the store. This made no sense. As I mentioned in the last paragraph, just as a bank robber will search for the weak link, a convenience store robber will search for his "weak link." Many stores are just begging to be robbed. The robber could stick a gun in the clerk's face under the cover of a Marlboro ad and nobody would be the wiser.

Many convenience store franchises have developed a store floor plan with this in mind. The register is at the front of the store, perpendicular to the window, so the clerk's profile is visible to the street. However, many small, independently owned stores have registers located in the back of the store and out of view. That's just crazy. Thus, if you own a retail store, please situate the register at the front of the store – preferably by the exit and visible from the street – and be done with it already!

#PY Tip 3: Hire a Security Guard: The professional security officer gets a bad rap. Often, they're viewed as minimum-wage know-nothings who have no authority to tell anybody what to do. Common slang nicknames include "rent-a-cop" or "wannabe" (referring to one who wants to be a police officer). Where does this lack of respect come from? From my experience, substandard guards encourage this derision due to the way they carry themselves. Either their uniform is sloppy, or they look completely disinterested in what they're doing. Even if these guards are experienced and competent, the fact that they don't appear to have it together gives the impression that they're unprofessional.

Photography courtesy of StudioOG.com

Why is the industry plagued by this type of guard? In many states, there are no requirements for becoming a guard. Most of the training and screening is dictated either by the insurance providers that insure the security agency or by past litigation. Like any business, the security company wants to avoid civil litigation or, if sued, minimize its financial impact. Ironically, to save money and maximize profits, the security companies do the bare minimum when screening and training their newest security personnel. Obviously, they're in business to make money, and to stay competitive they can't spend hundreds of dollars training an employee, especially if there's high employee turnover. In addition, the competition between companies in the security guard industry is fierce, and a company may be chosen simply because it was a dollar or two cheaper. This means the security company's pool of candidates is limited to those who will work for a lower rate of pay. The guard gets paid a dollar or two above minimum wage, and doesn't consider security work a long-term career. What's more, employee loyalty is almost non-existent. Guards are constantly looking for other opportunities to make more money and they frequently jump from company to company. When the client complains that their guard is lazy or indifferent to his assignment, my response is: "You get what you pay for!"

One summer in the 1990's when I was home from college, I got a job with a local security company (which has since gone out of business). I remember answering a job posting in a metro-west Boston newspaper. (The internet was not the job search vehicle it is today.) The next day I met with the director, who was a very nice gentleman and who represented the company very well. He wore the standard white shirt/black pants uniform and had a very comfortable office. Our pleasant conversation lasted about 30 minutes and I was hired. He made a copy of my driver's license, I completed a tax form and he handed me a sticky note. On the sticky note were two addresses: one for a medical facility so I could pee into a cup for a drug test and another that was the location of my first assignment. This was the extent of the screening process and orientation. I was 17 and excited to work without jumping through a lot of hoops. What makes me queasy today, however, is that many security companies still operate like this.

My first assignment with the company was a construction site where a new car dealership was being built. This assignment didn't require a lot of technical knowledge, equipment or specialized training. However, I didn't get so much as an employee manual, post orders or company policy (which, in retrospect, explains why the company is no longer in business). I subsequently worked for other security companies and learned both the good and the bad. I remember sitting for hours at a time on several different posts, thinking about the security company I would someday own. I contemplated what I would do differently. I'd be dedicated to screening, hiring and training dedicated professionals and would give guards direction, job expectations and ongoing training. Their duties and behavior would be dictated by post orders and employee manuals. I believe assignments should not involve depositing warm bodies somewhere to watch the grass grow but instead contain functions that provide a dedicated service to the client and reward professional demeanor and superior, professional guards.

Photography courtesy of StudioOG.com

CHAPTER SEVEN
ACCIDENTS HAPPEN

We've spent a good deal of time discussing intentional incidents that create victims, but what about when accidents happen – when you're the victim of an accident as a result of inattention or carelessness? The simplest illustration I can use is a motor vehicle accident. As a police officer, I respond to dozens of preventable motor vehicle accidents every month. Other officers, firefighters, tow operators and I all share glances and shake our heads. We've seen this type of accident a hundred times and we'll see it a hundred times more. Either the driver rolled through the intersection or paid no attention to the pedestrian when turning. Increasingly more common is that the driver was distracted by technology.

There was a time when cars were simple. They consisted of a transmission gear shift, heat or air condition switches and a radio with a cassette deck. Today, cars have become spaceships. Activating something no longer requires a simple knob or toggle switch. No, to change the radio station you need to launch a secret NASA code! What's worse, cars have a computer screen or digital display that creates a major distraction. Compound that with the small phone-sized computer in the pocket of every driver.

Unfortunately, the cause of motor vehicle accidents will continue to be distractions and there's nothing anybody can do about it. Car manufacturers follow supply and demand rules and will continue to provide these features as long as humans want them. In addition, due to privacy laws, accident investigators are required to obtain a warrant to view the history of one's phone in determining whether an accident was caused by texting. Also, several years ago President Obama signed into law the Driver Privacy Act, which prohibits an accident investigator from downloading the history of a vehicle's computer, called the Event Data Recorder (EDR). Not without probable cause or a warrant can the data be viewed for fear of violating one's "privacy"...give me a break!

Motor vehicle crashes are an example of the most common accidents you'll come across. Of course, there are careless people who work in all spectrums of life and who will cause accidents. The best tool a #PY Student can deploy is vigilance. Often, we trust people who have no business being trusted. We rely on government agencies to license nurses, barbers, plumbers, HVAC repairmen and home inspectors. Our assumption is that if they're licensed, they must be okay, right? WRONG! As the saying goes, "trust is good, knowing is better." I may trust those I hire to do their jobs, but I never relinquish control.

Several years ago, my oil burner broke down. It was, of course, winter and I was hard pressed to find a repairman to respond that day. A friend referred me to a local guy who responded quickly. I showed him the burner and asked him what he thought. This guy went into some explanation that might as well have been hieroglyphics reduced to speech. I figured, *Okay get it done*. During his visit, I checked in on him and asked him how it was going. I noticed the burner somewhat dismantled, with several parts on the ground. He was pleasant enough to provide an update and a forecast about his next procedure. About an hour later, I stopped in again and he was finished. The man explained to me what had happened, what parts he had replaced and what to expect for future maintenance. I asked several questions regarding carbon monoxide and other airborne poisons, and he reassured me that this was of no concern because everything was properly vented. Pretty simple, right?

Well, let me ask you: If I had left him alone and waited for him to return from the black abyss of my basement when he was done, do you think I would have obtained so much information? Would I have been able to see firsthand the parts on the floor and the burner dismantled? Would he have given me a status update part way through in addition to at completion? Probably not. In addition, any ending status report would not have included all the information in the middle.

So, why does this matter? Two reasons: First, the burner guy knew I was paying close attention to him. It's a known fact that people act differently if they presume they're being watched. This is precisely the reason why signs are posted at the entrance of department stores informing shoppers that the facility is equipped with surveillance cameras. In addition, anyone who has managed another human being knows that orders mean nothing unless they're followed up on. A manager can give all the orders she wants, but unless they're followed up on to determine whether they were completed, they're meaningless. In my example above, I followed up with burner man to ensure the job was being done.

Second, I showed an interest in what this guy did for a living. Most people care about what they do. They enjoy the opportunity to share their art. Thus, in my status report inquiry, I showed interest in what he did. I created a rapport, an unspoken bond with burner man and, in turn, he subconsciously wanted to do a good job for me. Thus, he was more likely to concentrate on quality work and not make mistakes. This minimized the opportunity for an accident. Sound stupid? Let me assure you: It is! But, that's how the human brain works and it can be applied to every aspect of your life.

#PY Exercise: Tomorrow, during your daily routine, stop and ask someone a specific question about what they do as they're doing it. This person can be the barista in the coffee shop, the IT guy in your office or the cop who just crossed your kid on the way to school. I assure you, if this is done genuinely and sincerely, and the person cares about what they do, they'll be more than happy to talk about it.

The theme of this chapter is to increase the requirements of your trust-o-meter. That doesn't mean trust nobody; it simply means to make those around you earn your trust. The mere fact that my burner guy was licensed meant nothing to me. The fact that he was referred by someone I trusted made the meter uptick a little. But the fact that he was able to explain what he was doing, explain what he had done and show his work allowed burner man to earn my trust.

#PY Tip: Accidents will happen. The following are steps we can take to avoid becoming victims of somebody's inattention or carelessness.

Step One: Be on high alert for anything out of the ordinary. Find the anomaly: something that just doesn't seem right and guard against it. For example, in our above traffic scenario, you would avoid the driver with the phone up to her face. Back off her bumper, or change lanes if you can. Stay on the sidewalk for another second if the guy is rolling through the stop sign. It may slightly increase your commute time but it's worth the extra couple of seconds.

Step Two: Leave nothing to chance. Your safety and the safety of those around you are paramount. Change the batteries of your carbon dioxide detector (in many ways, more important than your smoke detector). Cross the street if the construction crew has a crane over the street, just in case it falls. (This actually happened in Boston on April 3, 2006, when a crane fell onto a car and killed the driver.)

Step Three: Follow every tip, trick and suggestion in the following chapter.

CHAPTER EIGHT
VIOLENT CRIME

Statistically, you're more likely to be struck by lightning than to be the victim of a violent crime committed by a stranger. Most violent crime is committed by those we know. That may be difficult to understand, but much of today's violence is predicated by intense emotions. Intense emotions are commonly fueled by those to whom we have an emotional attachment. These include boyfriends, girlfriends, friends or even workmates. Violent crime may also be situational. For example, if a person is a drug dealer or user, they may find themselves in situations with less-than-reputable people. Drugs attract people who don't have much else. Violent crime is also ideological. Often, people are motivated to hurt others because they believe some higher power dictates it, because they enjoy it or because it's their belief that others have less worth than the suspect.

In this chapter, we will address that rare but most commonly feared type of violent crime: criminals who lurk around the corner or in the bushes. The reason we fear this violent attacker most is because the violence is random and difficult to explain. The media leads their evening broadcast with the story of the women who was kidnapped and tortured. My firsthand experience in media sensationalism happened several years ago, when I was the Public Information Officer of my police department. A woman was kidnapped just after midnight when she exited her cab and walked toward home. This became national news. Two intoxicated maggots found it necessary to physically grab her, throw her into their pickup truck and rape her. Needless to say, the media was all over this story. Breaking news at five o'clock, telling the story of another senseless crime. There is no explanation other than criminals looking for self-gratification and using a defenseless woman as their tool. That's it.

Thus, it becomes necessary for us to defend against this type of crime because it creates more fear than any other type of crime. Just as I laid out in my 2016 Ebook, *#Nationwide Police Strike,* fear of crime debilitates society:

The police agency's primary goal is met without anybody even realizing it: the citizen's fear of crime is reduced.

I hate to burst anybody's bubble (especially the hard-charging rookies), but reducing fear of crime is the single most important function of the police. Crime is going to happen whether you have one cop in town or a hundred. There is not much a police department can do to prevent crime from happening short of actively patrolling and being visible. However, officers can be trained, ready and alert in the event they're required to respond to those few and far between hot call incidents.

If during the common, community caretaking call, the officer is able to instill confidence that they're ready to respond at a moment's, notice they inevitably reduce fear of crime. Recent studies suggest fear of crime is more debilitating than crime itself. Ironically, most people who are victims of violent crimes tend to be younger because they often place themselves in unpleasant situations or are involved in more reckless behavior. However the people who fear crime the most are older citizens.

Thus, if police officers manage the symptoms (i.e., making arrests, conducting investigations, presenting well-documented cases to the district attorney), they ultimately cure the disease (fear of crime). And, frankly, that's all any American wants: to live our lives, enjoy our families without risk to our physical being or personal property. Reducing fear of crime is achieved by crime deterrence, crime suppression and crime prosecution.

So let's put this theory into perspective using poor Mrs. Jones. As a result of the officers' timely response, their professionalism and the positive resolution, Mrs. Jones feels great, protected and secure in her studio apartment. She now has confidence that if something worse were to actually happen, these great cops would respond and take care of business, ultimately reducing Mrs. Jones' fear of crime (and that of anybody else who hears her story).

Of course, the opposite is also true. If sloppy Joe-bad attitude cop arrives thirty minutes after the call and tells Mrs. Jones there's nothing he can do before driving away, Mrs. Jones' fear of crime skyrockets. She begins thinking, 'If this is the way I'm treated for a minor call, what will happen if something serious happens?' She then scrunches up her robe and draws the blinds.

However, much like its crime counterparts, *stranger violent crime* is preventable. With the proper mindset, tools and realization that today is not your day to be a victim, it's preventable. I've made my living watching human behavior. Starting as a security guard at a local mall and progressing to supervisor of a municipal police department, I know human behavior. I've watched all types of people from all walks of life go about in a state of unknowing. I call these people *urban zombies* – those who have their faces buried in their cell phones or who have headphones in their ears, walking down the street like the living dead. If people would wake up from their urban zombie state, they could react better, more effectively, and strike first before someone else gets the upper hand.

Mindset

Possibly the most important tool in your toolbox is the *proper mindset*. This principle is often used in other applications. At your spinning class, for example, the instructor encourages you by putting your mind in the frame of pushing yourself. In your art class, the teacher makes you stare at the blank canvass and imagine the painting before you dip the brush into the paint. Mindset prepares you to accomplish things you never thought possible – things others have done but about which you thought, *I could never do that*. It's imperative to imagine what you're going to do before it's necessary to implement it. Police officers play this game every day: "If X happens, I'll do Y."

In police training, as well as in other places, instructors teach "muscle memory." If you train this way, you'll react that way. During defensive tactics class or firearms training, for example, if your muscles are trained to pull out your weapon and grip it appropriately, your muscles will unconsciously react that way in a high-stress situation.

Several years ago, I was chasing a little Mazda sports car through a residential neighborhood. It was about three in the morning, so there was very little traffic. I knew the neighborhood like the back of my hand. As we continued on this particular road, I backed off slightly because I knew a tough corner was coming up. I let off the throttle as the Mazda hit the intersection at a high rate of speed (35 mph, if my bosses ask). Well, the Mazda hit the bump just before the intersection, went airborne and destroyed a pole and the neighbor's fence. The impact was as if a bomb had exploded. Smoke everywhere, pieces of wood falling from the sky and itty-bitty Mazda pieces on the ground. Before I knew it, I was at the passenger door with my Smith and Wesson aimed at the passenger's forehead. I thought to myself, *Where the hell did my gun come from?* In the excitement of the moment, my muscles instinctively pulled my weapon from the holster, gripped it appropriately and pointed in the direction of the threat. How did that happen? It happened because I had trained for several years, had the proper mindset and unconsciously performed the job.

Just as your muscles have a memory that snaps into action, your brain must be trained to recognize an issue and react as such. You accomplish this by following several simple steps. The first step is merely telling yourself that you're willing to do it! *If I'm attacked, I'll physically fight and I'll fight to win.* Make this assertion today, while reading this book. Look away from this page and say it: *I'm willing to fight, and I'll fight to win! I'm willing to fight and I'll fight to win!*

Next, physically practice going through the motions. Later in this chapter I will give you tips you can employ to fend off an attacker. Try them in your office, in your car or in your home. In slow motion, make a plunging motion, a kicking motion, a spinning motion. As you develop these movements, pick up the speed. If you can afford to take a private RAD (Rape Aggression Defense) class, I recommend it. These classes are unbelievably cost effective and mentally prepare students for such an event. However, it is not imperative to devote the time and energy when you can deploy different tactics today.

Think it can't happen to you? I'm sure the residents of the small community of Cheshire, Connecticut thought the same thing the day before July 23, 2007. With a population of about 30,000, Cheshire is a Norman Rockwell painting come to life – the quintessential New England town. The ladies of the Petit family (mom and two daughters) were followed home from the supermarket by two scumbags God should have thrown away a long time ago. To say these two were humans was a compliment. The family came home and did what any family does on the weekend. Just before bed, these two viruses broke into the home, tied up each occupant and did unspeakable things to the daughters.

At dawn, one scumbag escorted the mom to a bank to withdraw money while the other stayed behind to watch the captives. Soon after they returned, the scumbags realized Mr. Petit had escaped from the basement where he was being held. In a panic, the scumbags strangled the mom and lit the home on fire with both daughters inside, alive. In a veiled attempt to flee in the family car, the scumbags crashed into a police car and were apprehended while the Petit home burned to the ground.

Anybody with even a trace of a soul feels their stomach turn while reading about this family. There are more wrongs in this incident than one can sensibly comprehend. The purpose of my relating this story is for you to better understand why I offer the following tips.

#PY Tip 1: Look Him in the Face: A criminal scumbag approaches you from the rear. You hear his footsteps, you feel his presence. Most people in this situation would NOT turn around for fear of being rude. As I noted in an earlier chapter, most people still employ a sense of community when in this situation. Turning and looking someone in the eye would make for an awkward and uncomfortable situation. For fear of violating a societal norm, they restrain from shooting a quick *eye-shot*.

And remember, that's all an eye-shot is: a quick glance right at his eye. If he's a harmless Joe, no harm no foul. But if he's a scumbag, you may be able to divert a pending attack by just this one, simple move.

Our scumbag is hoping you'll act like 90 percent of the population would and recognize society's norms. The scumbag who commits this type of crime is easily recognizable and does not want you to see his face. At the same time, he's not going to wear a face covering (ski mask) so that he avoids drawing unwanted attention. He's put all his money on the fact that you're going to act a certain way. That includes not violating any societal norms (i.e., getting a good look at his face) or giving him a sincere fight.

#PY Tip 2: His Threats Are Just That: Threats: Even though our scumbag is able to overpower your resistance, he still wants you to comply. Cooperation makes his job easier. Thus, he tells you not to scream or fight back. He tells you to comply with his wishes. This is in the "Scumbag Manual." Ninety percent of the population would comply with his commands in an attempt to avoid further assault or injury. They assume that if they do everything they're told, they'll be rewarded with freedom. This assertion is false. This assertion also assumes that our scumbag is trustworthy, reasonable and sane. This is also wrong. Our scumbag is not stable, he is not reasonable, and most of all he is not truthful. All the rules of society, community and humanity are out the window! He is not a man of his word and he will not stay true to society's conventions, guaranteed! Welcome, you are now in the land of kill or be killed. Simple as that.

I would venture to guess that the Petit family made the same assertion: "I'll do exactly as they say and they'll be true to their word." I use the Petits' story as an illustration, not to Monday morning quarterback. Fight, fight and fight some more. Who knows? The mere introduction of resistance may make our scumbag reconsider from the onset. My argument: If I'm wrong, I'm not going down without a fight!

#PY Tip 3: Key to Freedom: In the next chapter, I will broach the subject of weapons. However, due to the availability and convenience of a variety of objects, I will direct your attention to a common item that can be deployed for self-defense. If you ever find yourself walking through an undesirable neighborhood or through a dark parking garage, you must take preemptive steps should the worst happen. Just before you exit the building, take out your car or house keys and hold them in your hand. Place the sharpest key on the ring between your index and middle finger so that the teeth are facing out when you make a fist.

Question: If the situation presents itself, would you be able to use this sharp instrument as a weapon? Can you picture yourself doing this? You should. As stated earlier, the first part of achieving any goal is to visualize yourself doing it. A friend once told me, "*It's not an achievable goal unless you write it down. Until then, it's only a dream.*" I love this saying and have adopted it in almost every facet of my life. Visualizing your intention sets the process in motion. It shapes and conditions your mindset. You're not a violent person; I know that. Violence is not in your nature; I know that as well. But as a reader of this book, I also know you will do anything possible to protect yourself.

Once you've conditioned your mindset and come to the realization that you'll do anything to fight and win, you're ready to use your *Key to Freedom*. With the key safely secured in your fist, teeth out and up, you need to drive that key into his eyeball in a punching/jabbing motion. Yes, his eyeball. Don't have a key? Your thumbnail works as well. You want to push that key like you're slicing an avocado. If you hit your mark and see or feel body liquid seeping or squirting, don't freak out. This is supposed to happen. And, of course, don't stop pushing into the avocado. Your plan is to push through the resistance, all the way to the core.

Have you ever seen those karate people attempting to break wood with their hands and for whatever reason it doesn't break? It's because they're pulling back ever so slightly just before their hand hits the wood. Their minds aren't set to follow through on the swing and the wood doesn't break. When puncturing your avocado, don't pull back. The thrust, jabbing, puncture motion should be fast and sure. No pulling back, no hesitation.

Once he's down and grasping for what's left of his eye, you'll disengage and run like your pants are on fire. If you did this process correctly, you may have to leave your key behind. Sorry, but that's just the way it is. You now need to stop reading this book for a second and look at the wall. Ask yourself, "Would I be able to drive a key into someone's eyeball, maiming him for the rest of his life?" Go ahead, I'll wait.

Several years ago, I was assigned to the Community Service Division of my police department. One of our functions was to communicate with local media outlets. Maintaining a great rapport with the local media is one thing my department does well. As I mentioned previously, one of my assignments was serving as Public Information Officer (PIO). I attended training and learned what I could and should not say about a specific case while being interviewed by the media.

In the beginning of this chapter, I told you the story of a horrific crime in which two scumbags kidnapped a woman and did unspeakable things to her. The woman was a college student who had been dropped off by a taxi several blocks from her home. As she proceeded home, the two men pulled beside her, jumped out and grabbed her. Due to the time of night and the commercial area she was in, nobody heard her scream and yell. The men drove her to a nearby parking lot and raped her.

When putting together the media statement, I wondered whether, if she had deployed her key to freedom, this could have been prevented. When they approached her, if she split the avocado of one of them, would this incident have happened? I really don't know. However, I want my #PY Students to avoid the same fate. Learn the key to freedom...split the avocado!

Tip #4: Attract as Much Attention as Possible: Moments before you implement your key to freedom, draw attention to yourself. Make noise with your voice or some other way. People are instinctively attracted to noises, especially an unusual vocal sound. Once the key is in as far as possible, run. Run as fast and as far as you can, yelling like your hair is on fire. Attract as much attention as possible. Even if you think nobody's around, yell anything that comes to mind. There are still good people in the world who want to help those in need. The guy sleeping in his parked car, the meter maid around the corner, even the coffee shop barista will hear you and come to your aid. Scumbags of this caliber are cowards. They want the path of least resistance and if you make it difficult for them, they may cut their losses and try another day.

Tip #5: Never Go for a Ride. If you're unable to fight off the initial attack and he attempts to put you in a conveyance or other mobile transport, you need to resist. Go back to tip #2, his social contract is meaningless. Put your mind in a place where his threats are trash. Whether or not you cooperate, this is what's going to happen to you, guaranteed. No matter what, don't get into the car.

The focus of your fight – kicks, punches – should be on the most sensitive part of his body. Yes, you guessed it; your focus is his sensitive *package*. Marine specialists say if you're ever attacked by a shark, you should dig your finger into its eye. Just as your key to freedom will set you free, your fingernails should be driven to the ball/genital area. You need to lock on with the grip of Satan and unleash holy hell. If you draw blood, all the better.

We've all seen the news stories about bodies being found in the woods near highways. How'd they get there? Were they killed before being placed into the car? Possibly. Were they walking down the highway and died in the woods? I don't think so. My contention is that they believed the criminal's word was reliable and cooperated with their scumbags. The victims were brought there while alive, then abused and murdered. Don't go for a ride.

CHAPTER NINE
WEAPONS

If one need protection, one needs only to possess a weapon. Ever hear that before? Although that may be true in some instances, possession of a weapon is not a panacea. Like with many areas in life, people often look to the easy answer: pop a pill, Google it, etc.

However, use of a weapon is not physically or mentally easy. As we discussed in the previous chapter, you need the proper mindset. You must be confident that if the situation presents itself, you'll act accordingly. In addition to knowing whether you can do it, you also need to know what you're doing.

For example, anybody can point a gun and press the trigger, right? Not exactly. I'm a licensed gun owner who enjoys the gun range and perfecting this skill. I've been working at it for the last 16 years and I've found there's a lot more to shooting a gun than "point and click." For this reason, I would never recommend that anyone arm themselves if they aren't experienced or even interested in learning the art of target shooting. Without proper training, experience and proficiency, that one round you fire in a dangerous situation will land in the side of a parked car, not in its intended target. That goes for a variety of other "per se" weapons listed in this chapter. So, although I'm a proponent of protecting oneself by any means necessary, I believe that carrying a weapon may not be the best option. And, as we've seen in the previous chapter, several items you already carry around can quickly be converted into weapons.

Guns

I will never be without a gun. My semi-automatic 40-caliber Glock goes where I go. It's the tool I've chosen to protect myself and my family. Rather, it was chosen for me. Before the police academy, I had never shot – nor even held – a gun. I remember that we started firearms training during week 18 of the academy. Because my name started with "D," I was the first volley of 10 officers on the line. We loaded up our magazines, charged our weapons and stood on the five-yard line. Staff Instructor Hickman directed us that at the sound of the whistle, we were to fire five rounds. I thought to myself, 'I don't want to be the first one to shoot, so I'll wait for everyone else to fire.' Apparently, everybody else thought the same thing. When the whistle was blown, not even a single shot rang out. Dead silence. Staff Instructor Hickman was furious. He blew the whistle again to signify cease fire and proceeded to ask us why nobody had fired their weapon. We burst out laughing when we realized we were all waiting for someone else to fire first. Staff Instructor Hickman tried to be mad but even he fought back a smile.

After that training in the academy and subsequent courses throughout my career, I've become unbelievably comfortable in the control, techniques and science of firearms. In fact, I became certified as a firearms instructor by the Massachusetts Police Training Council (MPTC) in 2009. Thus, it has become my chosen tool of defense. However, just as people have different preferences when it comes to pets, coffee or supermarkets, they have different preferences in terms of a defense tool. In many circumstances, obtaining and then deploying a firearm may be a reasonable option.

It should be noted that firearms can double cross their users if utilized haphazardly. For example, on July 14, 2006 a burglar alarm sounded in a home in Shrewsbury, Massachusetts. Thinking the man coming up the stairs was an unlawful intruder, the intoxicated homeowner took aim and fired his weapon toward the figure. When the dust settled, it was discovered that the so-called intruder was a police officer who had responded to the home's alarm system. The neighbor allowed police access after informing them the resident was away on vacation. As a result, the officer was injured by a single gunshot wound. He subsequently recovered from his injuries but soon after began suffering from post-traumatic stress disorder (PTSD). Officer Rice is no longer a police officer.

What's more taxing for the American citizen is the ongoing limitations some states have imposed to keep guns out of the hands of those who will misuse them. Although this is a noble quest, I'd venture to say that their attempts have been in vain. Even so, these states require licensing, training, and testing, which can become expensive.

#PY Tip: Find a Local Gun Range and Take a Class: Tell them you've never fired a gun before and you're curious about whether this is something you might like. Most ranges cater to those who have no experience and, frankly, enjoy teaching this skill to rookies. Don't be intimidated by employees at gun ranges. Most are good people who want you to become a good customer.

Electric Weapons

Massachusetts has some of the strictest laws with regard to weapons. Those weapons that the legislative branch of the government claims to be too dangerous to possess are commonly referred to as "per se" weapons. These weapons include stilettos, dirk knives, brass knuckles and, of course, electrical weapons (aka, stun guns). Under Mass general law chapter 140 section 131J, one cannot possess or sell an electric weapon, with the penalty being up to two-and-a-half years in jail. However, a recent United States Supreme Court decision said that the Massachusetts law is unconstitutional! Thus, a law that police have been enforcing for decades has been nullified due to this decision. What's important for the #PY Student is that police departments are educating their officers to NOT arrest for this crime.

According to a thetruthaboutguns.com article posted on March 21, 2016: *The case at bar, Jamie Caetano v. Massachusetts involved a defendant — a 4'11" woman residing in the Commonwealth of Massachusetts — who had been given a stun gun by a friend for the purposes of protecting herself against an abusive ex-partner, who was also the father of her two children. Caetano had allegedly been beaten previously by her ex so severely as to require medical attention.*

This Supreme Court decision has had dramatic implications in the area of self-protection and self-preservation. One could make the argument that, under this decision, all types of weapons that are currently banned for being per se could be legalized. Thus, one could argue that stilettos, dirk knives and even "brass knuckles" can be possessed for the purpose of protecting oneself. A person who rides the train late at night can now legally protect herself with a tool that works.

Knives

I have a drawer of folding knives in my basement. I've collected them over the years with no real purpose. I have no training, skills or even interest in learning defensive moves with a knife. Of course, many people view the possession and implementation of knives just as I view firearms. They train with them, all the while perfecting this skill. They are professionals.

I, on the other hand, am not. Thus, I would never carry one unless I was fishing or working in a warehouse with boxes. It should be noted that I hate the water and my career trajectory does not have "warehouse worker" in its immediate future (I hope). However, some believe that if a folding knife is in their purse or on their belt, they'll be able to deploy it and make their escape. To them I say: Do it! To everyone else, I argue that carrying a knife has a downside. For example, you're attacked and it's an all-out struggle with Scumbag Jimmy. You remember that you have your trusty knife in pocket, and you begin fishing around for it. Once you get a hold of it, your other hand assists in its opening (because you know a spring-assisted switchblade is illegal). Once you open it, you begin to plug away at the torso. Sounds reasonable enough, but it's not practical. By the time you fish it out and deploy it, you've already lost. Scumbag Jimmy has already pinned you down or is a mile down the street with your wallet.

There's yet another concern I have about the deployment of knives. Several years ago, I was working the overnight shift in a two-man unit affectionately referred to as the "U-car." Officer Sean Russell and I had just cleared a call and stopped at 7-Eleven on Park Drive. After we parked, we noticed a large gathering on the sidewalk. As we approached, we could see that the group was huddled around a person lying on the ground. It appeared that the group had recently formed and was in a panic/stunned state. I shouted to Sean to grab the medical kit and I pushed my way through the crowd. The man on the ground appeared to be a Hispanic/Latino male in his mid-20s. He was unconscious, his eyes were rolled back into his head and he was suffering from agonal respiration.

Leaning over this male was another 20-something male who appeared to be in distress. He was yelling several dramatic commands, which included “Don’t die,” among others. I remember thinking to myself, ‘This looks like a scene out of the movie *Boyz ‘n the Hood*.’ I asked him, “What happened?” Once my weeping friend took a breath, he said he and his “homeboy” had just fucked up some white dude(s). He proceeded to lift the injured man's shirt and I observed a small, one-inch puncture wound in his lower left abdomen. It struck me as odd that the wound looked like an opening, with no blood or bodily fluids. What we later realized was that he was bleeding internally. I proceeded to check the victim for other injuries by lifting his shirt to his collar. Of course, there were several more of these puncture wounds in his chest.

Officer Russell and I performed CPR, loaded him into the ambulance and sent him to the hospital. Several hours later, we learned the man had died. Apparently, one of the stabs had punctured his lung as well as several other vital organs and the doctors couldn't save him.

As all good cops do, once the victim was loaded into the ambulance, Officer Russell and I began our investigation. Several of the huddled onlookers informed us that the incident had not happened at that location. Homeboy pulled our victim out from the back seat of a white car that was curbside and on the sidewalk. We later learned that the incident had happened in Cambridge, a city just over the Mystic River. My wailing friend loaded his buddy into the white Chevy and attempted to drive him to the hospital. Homeboy became lost and decided the best course of action was to pull to the side of the road and yell for help. It was a cliché case of nonverbal indication of guilt: Homeboy knew he was wrong, so he chose to flee (but I'll explain that later).

What had happened was a bad combination of alcohol and testosterone. A Harvard graduate student by the name of Alexander Pring-Wilson was walking back to his dorm when he and the "victim" had an exchange of words. The real cause of the altercation will never be known. However, a good case of "turn the other cheek" would have been in order. Nevertheless, the three of them got tangled in a bowl of male stew. While in the thick of the fight, Pring-Wilson unfolded his trusty Swiss army knife. In what can only be described as a rash of upward, jabbing motions, Pring-Wilson caught the victim several times. Whether the victim knew he was stabbed when they returned to the car is unknown; however, the pair jumped into the white Chevy and drove off.

The rest is history. Cambridge Police located Pring-Wilson and charged him with murder. Two trials (which included my testimony) and several appeals later, Pring-Wilson pled guilty and was sentenced to two years in jail. In addition, in March of 2012, he was ordered by the Mass Civil Court of Appeals to pay the victim's daughter $250,000 in damages. Justice Thomas P. Billings ruled the following:

"[Pring-]Wilson's intent, in pulling out his knife and using it as he did, was not to kill or even to inflict serious injury on either of his assailants; it was to drive them away. In so doing, however, he was negligent: first, in failing to avail himself of reasonable alternatives to combat, and second, in employing more force than was reasonably necessary to repel the attack. On the last point, the number of knife wounds inflicted, and particularly the nature of the fatal wound, were disproportionate to the danger actually posed or reasonably apprehended."

Unreal, truly unbelievable.

What the judge was essentially saying was that it was unnecessary for Pring-Wilson to deploy a knife when he could've clunked their heads together like Moe. What is the takeaway from this story? As I've reiterated throughout this chapter, use only the amount of force necessary to assure your escape. Had Pring-Wilson been a 4'11" female rather than a 6'2" man, this case would have had a different outcome. Is that fair? Of course not. But as my mom always says: "Life isn't fair!" Whether you agree is inconsequential; what you need to remember is that if a knife is the weapon with which you've chosen to defend yourself, make sure it's legal to carry, its readily accessible and your intention is just enough to escape. Once your escape is possible, stop the upward thrusts. If you overlook these important recommendations, you'll find yourself answering a plea to the judge.

Yours truly testifying in the Pring-Wilson case. Courtesy of Court TV.

Weapons of Convenience

Almost anything you pick up is considered a weapon. I've had cases in which a beer bottle was smashed over an opponent's head. My favorite was a family incident in which the dangerous weapon was a grapefruit. In Massachusetts, as in many other states, the crime of *Assault and Battery by means of a Dangerous Weapon* refers to anything one can use to injure another human being. Of course, when used in self-defense (or defense of another), the item is no longer a weapon, it's a defense mechanism. This, of course, is only my opinion, though I'm confident any judge worth her salt would agree with me.

Just as a previous chapter discussed your key to freedom, you can deploy any weapon of convenience to defend yourself. This is legal as long as your intent is to create distance and escape. After that's accomplished and you've explained yourself, the cop will offer you a high-five. Always remember, however, that there's a fine line between defending yourself by use of a defense-mechanism and going on the offensive. Your intention to get away should not be clouded by a desire for revenge. For example, after you employ your key to freedom and he goes down, you must fight the urge to release your anger on the back of his head. This usually results in head holes that probably shouldn't be there. Many courts, judges and prosecutors will frown on this activity, though of course I'll be cheering for you!

CHAPTER TEN
SCENARIO

Now let's put everything you've learned into a series of demonstrative scenarios. I'll provide the scene and the event. Before you read the options, quickly think about what you would do in that situation. This is a critical step in the process because most people don't play the "what-if" game. The more you practice the what-if game, the more quickly and effectively you'll respond to different intense situations. After you've done this, read the following choices and choose one. Read the result of the option you've chosen and determine whether it seems like the right choice. If not, go back to the choices and choose another. Keep doing this until you've found the right option for you.

Remember, there's no right or wrong answer. This exercise is intended to help you think critically about your reaction. In addition, it's to help you begin thinking about your safety in everyday situations and, thus, to never drop your guard. Listen to your instinct – or, better, your little (wo)man – and act accordingly. Let's begin.

Scenario one: You reside in a two-story colonial home and are awakened in the middle of the night by a loud pounding at the front door. The banging is so intense, the picture frames are dancing against the wall. You quietly slide out of bed, peek through the blinds and see two masked men giving your door the once over. One of the men is driving his shoulder into your door like Refrigerator Perry would for the '85 Bears. The other provides the door with the occasional front kick with his foot. Although you've already read this book and applied the necessary precautions in dead bolting the door, you realize it's only a matter of time before they get in. Your two kids and significant other are safely tucked away in dreamland and haven't heard a thing. If you attempt to make an escape out the back door, you'll have to pass by the front door. They may see you through the window and be scared off, or they may be extra motivated to "get you!" Also, by the time you wrangle the little ones, these burglars may have gained entry and meet you at the front door.

Thus, their flight or fight will kick in and you've just put your family in harm's way. What do you do?

Options

Option A: Go for it. Scoop up the kids, make a break past the entry point and head for the back door.

Option B: Wrangle up the family and lock everybody in the master bathroom. Hope they just want the goods and move on.

Option C: Load the pistol, perch yourself at the top of the stairs and empty your magazine at entry.

Option D: Climb out a window to freedom.

Results

Result of Option A: You're able to quietly wake the family, tiptoe down the stairs and past the front door. As you're making your way through the kitchen, the wood splinters and the scumbags make their way into your home. Fortunately, they don't see you as you slip out the back and run to the neighbors' house. This option works only if you're fast. It takes less than 30 seconds for a seasoned burglar to break in a door. It took you about 15 seconds to figure out what was happening and probably another 15 to alert the others. My guess is, you more than likely don't have enough time for this option.

Result of Option B: You quietly slide the youngins out from under the covers and go back to the master bathroom. You lock the door and huddle in the bathtub. The front door explodes open and the scumbags enter. This option works only if the scumbags' intended target is property and not the occupants (you). I, for one, am not comfortable enough taking that chance. As a police officer, I believe everybody is out to get me. Let's face it, I arrest scumbags who deserve to go to jail, not the priest at Sunday mass. Many of these losers don't have much to lose. Thus, although a viable option for some, it's not for me.

Result of Option C: To assume these scumbags who worked ever so hard to get into your home are interested in property is crazy. You have two cars parked in the driveway, the lawn is cleanly kept and the porch light is still on: Scumbag Charlie knows someone is inside. Thus, my first thought would be that these guys are coming to hurt someone. So, option C is probably for me. I can picture several of my gun range friends reading this right now who are loving option C (you know who you are).

After you hear the bang and observe the scumbags, you do as you would in option B and gather your family in the bathtub. You open the wall safe and load your semi-automatic Smith and Wesson. You kneel at the top of the stairs, keeping your gun at the low ready. You remind yourself, *This will be deployed only if one of these scumbags attempts an ascent to the upper level of my home*. At first glance, Charlie Scumbag can't see you. He then rounds the corner and starts jogging up the stairs. His face is covered by a ski mask and due to the limited visibility, you can't tell whether he's holding something. However, with the level of violence he has already shown, you're confident that if he reaches your loved ones in the bathtub, he intends to do them harm. Thus, you release a double tap (two rounds) center mass. The dark figure has completed his ascent and is now on a quick descending trajectory.

One of two things results from the sound of gunfire: The other scumbag flees your home like a rat from a sinking ship or he's so determined to inflict pain, he's still willing to engage. If the latter is true, don't panic. Take a deep breath and keep the weapon steady. You have the advantage because of your height and the lack of light. In addition, due to the narrowness of the stairwell, the scumbags' ascent up the stairs will be single file. The staircase becomes a tunnel of death, dropping scumbags as they run up the stairs.

Result of Option D: This is a viable option assuming the second floor of your home is not too high. Some homes have windows that overlook another roof (like in the television show “3rd Rock from the Sun”). If this is the case, I would say that this is a very reasonable option. However, if you’re dropping kids onto the patio, I’d think twice.

Scenario Two: You’re shopping for new clothes at Walmart. Your brain is so focused on the new Superman shirt for Jimmy, you don't see Scumbag Charlie sneaking around you. He’s been eyeing you for the past 15 minutes and now he’s decided to act out his urges. The aisles in this Walmart are narrow and merchandise seems to be a free-for-all pile, so it’s not uncommon for the occasional bump or sideswipe between two shoppers. You then feel Scumbag Charlie invading your radius. Your right shoulder has met his right shoulder as he viewed the shirts on the rack behind you. What is your next course of action?

Options

Option A: Fight or flight, you give scumbag Charlie a quick jab with your elbow to create distance.

Option B: Quick eye-shot, you give Scumbag Charlie an eye-shot hoping this is enough.

Option C: Fight or flight, you leave the shirt where it is and move farther down the aisle.

Option D: You ask him a question: "You like this shirt?"

Results

Result of Option A: The quick jab takes him by surprise and disrupts his game. His prior victims never engaged him like this. He then takes the hint and moves on. This is a viable option but only if Scumbag Charlie is, in fact, a *scumbag* and not just Regular Charlie. Most men (including me) would interpret a quick jab of the elbow as indicating that the person who offered it is a crazy shopper who likes her space!

Result of Option B: You attempt a quick eye-shot but Scumbag Charlie isn't one for eye contact so your eyes never meet. However, he does sense that you're looking at him and it's enough to disrupt his game. Most of his victims don't realize he's on top of them until it's too late. However, you're a #PY Student and radius aware. Thus, he realizes you aren't to be messed with and he moves on.

Result of Option C: You note where the Superman shirt is and flee the area. You need to pick up a few more things, so you plan to come back later. However, Scumbag Charlie isn't giving up and continues to follow you through the store. Thus, you may have to deploy one of the other options.

Result of Option D: You raise the shirt to his face and ask, "You like this shirt?" Scumbag Charlie is so thrown off his game, he's catatonic. You persist in your inquiry and he returns with a "Oh, yeah...very nice." You make sure you maintain eye contact the entire time, not as a friend but more as teacher who just busted a kid smoking in the bathroom. This part is crucial because you don't want to give him the impression that you're actually interested in his opinion or that you're warm for his form. If executed well, you've disrupted Scumbag Charlie's game again and he decides to move on.

Scenario Three: It wasn't the boss who kept you late, but the ongoing desire to get the job done. Everyone else called it quits hours ago and is probably home watching prime-time television while snuggling with their cats. You power down the Mac and head for the door. Your brain is consumed with not only what you've just achieved, but also when you're going to fit in food and sleep before it's time to come back. While sorting this out, you exit the building and walk through the parking lot. The one car in the lot looks so lonely, you laugh to yourself. That's when an unknown figure wraps you in a bear hug from behind. Your natural bodily reaction is to lurch forward in an awkward dry heave of the torso. The man says something close to your head, but in this moment, you're too busy to understand the English language. You've come to the grim realization that you've just become a victim of the worst type of crime American society can fear. With this reality in hand, you now have several important decisions to make.

Options

Option A: You attempt to hear scumbag out and listen to his demands. You decide that whatever he wants, he gets and you're confident that whatever he promises will be delivered.

Option B: You conduct an all-out feline scramble to obtain freedom. Have you ever picked up a cat that didn't want to be held? You do that. There's no knee, elbow or fist you won't use.

Option C: You listen to Loser Larry and advise him that you'll cooperate with his demands. However, you find an opportunity to take advantage of his confidence and make a break for it.

Option D: You concentrate on his genitals. You deploy a little of option B with all your attention on his groin and other sensitive areas of the body.

Results

Result of Option A: You do as he says and give in to his perverted fantasies. He allows you to walk away knowing you've seen his face, car, etc. or he kills you.

Result of Option B: You make it unbelievably difficult for him to maintain a hold on you. He attempts to regain control by hitting you in the head, but you're moving so fast. He misses and you're able to break free from his grasp. You run to your car, hit the unlock button and you're in. His plan is foiled and he goes back to his mother's basement.

Result of Option C: He walks you back toward the building and behind a shrub. He tells you this is what he wants you to do and you oblige, forever looking for the right opportunity. You see it and take it. You're able to create some distance, all the while focusing on the task at hand, and are able to get to your car.

Result of Option D: This is the option my wife would take. In fact, she introduced this escape route to me several years ago. (No, I was not Loser Larry.) Most women have long fingernails for aesthetic reasons, but they can also play a vital role in ensuring safety. Let's say Loser Larry takes you back toward the building like in option C and exposes his private area for your observation pleasure (or whatever perverts do). You, in turn, use those aesthetically pleasing fingernails to drive deep into this region. I would focus the index and middle fingers' attention on the undercarriage and the thumb to the trunk. Grossed out yet? Good. Remember, if you can't picture it, you can't do it. Then, commence a death grip to this area as hard as you can. If you rush the initial gouging process, it'll just become a superficial wound as opposed to its intended purpose. When blood appears, this means it's working. Don't let up now!

You should know that while you're driving your manicure into his groin, you may receive a blow or two to the head. This reaction from Loser Larry is understandable. Even though it'll hurt, it shouldn't distract you from your directive. Once you've held your grasp for 10 seconds or so, pull in a downward thrusting motion, taking as much skin as you can. Don't pull back like you're taking off a shoe. No, pull down like you're pulling the stuffing out of a turkey's hindquarters.

#PY Exercise: So, what do you think? Were you able to think critically about specific situations and whether you'll be willing to react? Begin thinking about your safety in everyday public exposure situations and determine whether you're able to maintain your guard. Can you feel your instinct – or, better yet, your little man – communicate? Will you be able to act accordingly?

CHAPTER ELEVEN
CONCLUSION

When I started this project, I figured I put some helpful tips down on paper and publish it on Amazon Kindle. I figured I'd tell some anecdotal stories to illustrate some key points and make someone laugh. But as I spoke to more people about my book idea the more I learned and the more I had to contribute. I learned a lot about how some feel when alone and how they go about protecting themselves. I spoke to colleagues who teach self-defense classes to get their perspective about what a student should learn. I never thought the end result would be this book.

I hope you found it interesting enough to share with others. Feel free to lend this book to friends and family. Making money with books was never my intention. My goal is to help you Protect Yourself and help others protect themselves.

The intent of this book was to provide tips and tricks to protect you from the most common types of victimization. It goes without saying that anything contained within should only be used for lawful purposes. Freemasons have an ancient sign for cases when they need help from their fellow members. Masonic tradition teaches this sign only be used in extreme cases of danger or distress. You now have the obligation to use what you’ve learned responsibly.

We live in a society with a need to take a broader look at our physical security. Unfortunately, many grown adults live their lives with blinders on to society's criminals. Those who prey on the vulnerable, on the weak, on those who aren’t prepared to protect themselves. This does not just apply to Americans or any other country, but to the human race. We have become dependant on technology and government to protect us, almost relinquishing control to others. We need to take ownership for our own safety. Humans are animals with free will. Some feed on others even if it only temporarily benefits them.

I hope I was able to answer questions while providing tips and tricks to take common sense, proactive steps to protect yourself. Apply what you've learned in this book today. Begin by taking a walk around your home with a notepad and write a list of my so-called pre-historic tools. These have been in existence since the birth of man and is the simplest form of protecting yourself.

Be aware of your radius. Take a self-defense course and practice physical moves. Continue to read and learn as much as you can because your safety should never be left to others. Friend me on Facebook (Rob Disario), visit my website RobDisario.com and attend one of my upcoming speaking engagements. In our communications, challenge me! You face these challenges everyday and I learn from #Protect Yourself students who will stop at nothing to win! Thank you for your support and we'll see you out there.

ABOUT THE AUTHOR

Robert J. Disario is a sergeant for a police department just outside Boston, Massachusetts. He is currently assigned to the patrol division, where the blue lights frequently go on. After receiving a bachelor's degree in criminal justice from the University of Hartford in 2000, Rob graduated from the Lowell Police Academy, a MPTC certified police academy in Massachusetts, and began work in the public sector. In June, 2009 he was promoted to the rank of sergeant, through which he facilitated and supervised thousands of criminal investigations.

With this experience Rob has developed the Protect Yourself philosophy. Rob's goal is to share his knowledge, experience and techniques so everyone can protect themselves. Please visit RobDisario.com for other publications, upcoming speaking engagements, signing events, free downloads and to sign up for the #PY newsletter.

COMING SOON
BECOMING A COP

The following is the first two chapters of Rob's upcoming book Becoming a Cop. Due to be released in 2018, this informational book is ideal for anybody considering a career in law enforcement. Please contact Rob with your impressions. Thank you and enjoy!

From the Author of #Nationwide Police Strike

BECOMING A COP

What You Need to Know Before Taking the Job

Robert J. Disario

CHAPTER ONE
INTRODUCTION

I've spent my entire adult life learning about law enforcement. I began as a child watching and mimicking Ponch and Jon on the 1970's television show "ChiPs". I spent the majority of time as a teenager dreaming of riding around in a police cruiser chasing bad guys, conducting traffic stops and enforcing the law. I started working as a Security Guard for a company called D.B. Kelly in 1997 when law enforcement was a vague dream in my mind. I spent my college career learning theories of crime, society and police. After my bachelors' degree in criminal justice, I trained to be a police officer in the police academy. I've dedicated the rest of my life, to this point, actually doing the job of a police officer. As crazy as it may sound, after all that time, money and training, I still don't know all I should know about being a police officer. Everyday I put the uniform on I learn something new and that's what makes this career one of the best in the world.

I constructed this manuscript because I always thought there should be a guidebook that offers the nuts and bolts, the skeleton and the bare bones of what the actual job of a police officer entails. Everything I learned in college was theoretical. The information attempted to explain why society acts the way it does and why the police respond the way they do. In the police academy they taught specific laws, rights of arrest as well as how to physically defend myself when the worst happens. However, none of what I read prepared me for what the job is really all about. Not to say either of these programs (college or academy) was unimportant, they're extremely imperative, but in order to build a house one needs to start with a foundation. Thus this guide is the foundation for your law enforcement career structure.

In the short time it takes you to read this guide you will be as prepared to be a police officer as if you spent four years in an accredited, criminal justice college program. My intention is not to minimize the lessons by which college can teach, but to supplement the information it provides and relate to the real world occupation. Even though it is beneficial, fifty minutes in a classroom three times a week to learn theories about society is not what police work is all about.

Ideally, this book should be read by a high school or college student who is considering a career in law enforcement. This guide will also prepare a prospect that has been hired by a police department and is currently enrolled, just finished or has yet to start the academy. This material may also be useful to the younger, rookie police officer who is still in the early years of their career.

This guide is organized so that it touches the most important issues in real world policing. As you read you'll find the information is vastly different that what you might see on television, however it explains why the officers in shows like Fox's Cops do what they do. This point is exemplified by the examples I use from my own work as a patrolman. I offer examples that best illustrate the point that I'm trying to make. Even though they may be slightly entertaining (I hope), the stories are not meant to be entertainment. They are simple examples of what the typical police officer, from both a large city and small town will face.

While assigned to the Community Service Division I have spent a large amount of my time training. I have prepared valuable material in an effort to teach veteran officers during 'in-service' training. This material is taught in such a manner that can be easily applied on the street by my students. Those students usually apply what they've learned within a matter of hours, therefore my lessons are simplified so that the information is easily understood, learned and subsequently applied. I have used this style of teaching in this guide, so that even the novice learner can understand and easily apply what they've learned.

Throughout each chapter, I use terms such as "you", "he" and "his" for mere simplicity and not to imply "he" is the only one that can do the job. I use the term "the good patrolman" to explain what the proper tactic or proper behavior is and to decipher the difference between a typical 'police officer' and an exceptional police officer. I use phrases such as "you will have to" and "you must be" so not confuse the reader with nonsense jargon and thus make it more accessible to the lay person, whom this information is directed.

At the end of each chapter is both a 'What You Need to Know' and 'Discussion Questions' section to summarize and reinforce the subject matter. Also, in small boxes along the way are fun historical facts about policing, police departments or other related topics. Be sure to read and share these fun facts with others.

So please enjoy this guide and share it with anybody and everybody because knowledge and information is only useful to those who want it.

What You Need to Know

I. This is and nuts and bolts manual explains what the job of a police officer actually entails.

II. This guide is organized so that it touches the most important issues in real world policing.

III. I use terms such as “you”, “he” and “his” for mere simplicity and not to imply “he” is the only one that can do the job.

CHAPTER TWO
THE BASICS

There are three skills a police officer is required to have. The officer has to either naturally have each skill or have the capacity to learn and implement these skills to be an effective patrolman. The following is a list of skills and the question one should ask himself to illustrate why that particular skill is of vital importance:

I. **Observation skills**: Is he going to kill me?

II. **Communication skills**: Can I convince him not to kill me?

III. **Defensive self-preservation:** If he tries to kill me can I protect myself?

I. Observation skills are probably the most important skill a police officer has because simply we are trained, paid observers. When on free patrol a patrolman must be constantly combing through the windows of the cruiser. It just doesn't include the windshield. A good patrolman will rotate his head from left to right and into each mirror. People who see him should ask themselves, 'what is that cop looking for?' This behavior should begin the minute the officer leaves the back parking lot of the station until he pulls into the lot at the end of eight hours. You can understand how tired the good patrolman is at the end of his shift from constantly moving their eyes, head and absorbing his environment. Those who are not fatigued need to ask themselves, am I a good patrolman?

So what are you looking for? The patrolman is looking for "the anomaly," anything out of the ordinary, anything that just doesn't look right. That draws the question, how do I know if it doesn't look right? Well the good patrolman knows his route. He knows the nuances, the businesses, the routines of people, cars and structures. That's why police management (hopefully) will assign officers to a specific route in which they will work everyday. If during the course of your career you have a supervisor who refuses to assign officer to a route, you can be sure he's not a very good supervisor. I will review police supervisors in the chapter 'organization'.

When you observe something that just does not

seem right you must look further into the issue and thus using more of your observation skills. Upon closer inspection, is this behavior you are witnessing really odd or unusual or does it ‘check out?’ The majority of the time, even though it looks out of the ordinary, it will check out and will be nothing criminal. However don’t let that frustrate you, I would rather check it out and be nothing than not looking deeper and having it be a crime in progress. Remember the job is only fun when you come into contact with the criminals.

Observation skills also come into play when responding to a call for service. While responding to a crime in progress the good patrolman will absorb his environment. He will pay special attention to cars speeding away or pedestrians walking from the crime scene. Surprisingly enough, the dispatcher will not give you all the information you might need while responding. Descriptions of people involved or makes and models of cars don’t get dispatched until after you arrive at the scene. So pay particular attention to people’s reaction at the sight of a police car or to the arrival of a police officer on scene. Most people will go about their business without more than a single glance, but a person who has just committed a crime is aware they will be of interest to the police. Their reaction will be odd and their behavior will strike you as strange. The criminal will give your cruiser several looks over their shoulder and trying to decide when he should start running. The criminal knows where you are going and wants to know if he caught your eye as you drove by. Because of this paranoia, their body language is unconscious and is an obvious benefit to the police.

A police officer should also be able to quickly process information and compute into a language so in the event he observes similar information with his eyes he can recognize it. For example, if the dispatcher broadcasts a description of a suspect or missing person, the good patrolman should be able to recognize when they see it. What I always tried to do is while the dispatcher is talking, I build the person in my head. I picture the jeans, the white t-shirt with the hair color and race. What I try to not do is add the easily removable articles of clothing such as glasses or hats. These types of items are easily picked out of a crowd but can mislead even the good patrolman in thinking he's not our man. What you want to do is focus on the things a suspect can not change.

Observation skills go beyond just sight. All of a patrolman's senses are important and should not be dismissed. What you hear is sometimes more important that what you see. For example, when answering a call at a residence of domestic disturbance or other type of disturbance, stand at the front door for a second before knocking. Stand to the side of the door frame, so not to be in the line of fire of stray rounds or bullets meant for responding police. Turn your radio down to low or even off, and put your ear close to the door. Sometimes what is heard by arguing residents can be extremely helpful in determining what is really happening before the residents know that the police have arrived.

Another technique to assist with sense of sound is leaving the driver's side window of the cruiser open. While on free patrol I always open the drivers' side window at least a couple inches so that I can hear someone is shouting for help at the sight of a police car. A cruiser traveling thirty miles an hour takes a split second to pass the opening of an alley, but that's just enough time to hear a sign of distress. In the winter I turn the heat up and roll down the window about half way and my ear will picks up street noise. I have trained my ear to be able to distinguish the difference between children playing in a playground and a plea for help.

Your sense of smell can come in handy when diagnosing one's sobriety or whether they have just inhaled a controlled substance. It has always amazed me that when approached by a police officer, even the most drunk guy will straighten up and try to play it off like he's sober. Sometimes they'll even do a pretty good job, except for the fact that they smell like they just bathed in beer.

Smell also comes in handy when neighbors complain of a 'strange' odor coming from an apartment next door. A seasoned patrolman or firefighter can recognize the stench of death the moment the elevator doors open. I've responded to sudden deaths where the time of death was determined to be both an hour ago and several months ago. Even though I knew what is behind the door to the bedroom it is my responsibility to kneel beside the lifeless body and check for any sign of life. I know it sucks, but that's the job. On several occasions I knelt next to a person who was reported to be dead and was shocked to learn the person wasn't dead at all. The person was lying in a pool of both blood and human excrement and by all accounts appeared to have passed on. That's why it is so very important to go the extra mile and check their vital signs. When I started this job I remember thinking that that kind of stuff is why we have paramedics or firefighters, but I shortly realized I arrived to the victim's side even before the fire department got out of bed.

Your sense of smell can also help when searching for suspects in a home especially in the winter. Suspects running from the police tend to be people who are not in shape for that type of exercise. The threat of being caught causes ones stress level to increase, also causing their heart rate to increase, therefore they sweat and create body odor. When the windows of a home are closed the suspect hiding under a box or behind a pile of clothes can give off a brutal stench. Just follow the stench and you'll find your man.

The fact observation skills will save an officers life makes it the most important skill of what you need to know to be a police officer. 'Is he going to kill me?' is the question used to illustrate its importance. 'He' refers to a police officer's adversary. A good patrolman can answer this question by merely observing an adversary. Body language is the medium that acts out what the brain is thinking. If the adversary is holding a knife and charging at you with a face of pure aggression, chances are he wants to kill you. This is an obvious example, but the good patrolman will pick up on more subtle observations. And, as previous stated, a police officer should use all four senses: sight, sound, touch, and smell.

II. Communication skills are of similar importance, however they are a tool that either comes easily and genuine or difficult and patronizing. Knowing when to deploy this tool is also important so not to put a band-aid on a broken leg. For example, if one was aggressively charging at you with a baseball bat, your response would not be to discuss the matter with him to have him realize the errors of his ways. That would just be dumb. On the flip side, if a person was sitting in the fetal position on the floor, suffering from depression and looking for guidance, the good patrolman doesn't pull his weapon and order him to the ground. Therefore when it comes to policing, there is a delicate balance to know when to communicate and when to respond with a tactical advantage.

The act of communication is done by every life form known to man. The whales communicate deep below the sea with moaning sounds and birds do it from the tallest branches of the tallest trees. Humans learn how to communicate from watching our parents talk "baby" to us in the crib. We develop this skill between our friends with slang words and phrases and then perfect this skill as a professional through formal education. However, when it comes to police work communication takes on a whole new meaning. The patrolman uses this skill on every single call, whether it is a service or emergency response the officer needs to become proficient with this skill less he become ineffective. As you move on in your career, you will find if you are unable to speak intelligently with another, either the victim or suspect, your calls will become a complete debacle. You will devote more time to get the situation under control then it would take to learn how to communicate well. What will result is your colleagues and your supervisor will anticipate that every call you respond to will be a disaster and they will plan accordingly. Your fellow patrolman will not assist you on any calls unless they are dispatched to the same location. This is because they want to avoid getting mixed up with a citizen complaint or disciplinary action when you screw up. When your fellow patrolman refuse to back you up it becomes an officer safety concern. Your supervisor will either keep you on a short leash or watch your every move. He will assign you to a job that will keep you out of trouble and let me assure you, you do not want that job.

O.k., so how does one communicate effectively? Many books have been written to try answer this very question, but I offer the nuts and bolts explanation for the good patrolman. First, communication is two fold, speaking and listening and in police work the latter is invaluable. Sometimes people, who call the police or get into trouble with the police, just want to be heard. And it's funny how different people act after they have told their side of the story and your response is actively listening to what they had to say. "Actively listening" means that as someone is speaking you're not just staring at someone with a stupid, blank stare. Actively listening is body language. When I listen to someone, I tilt and nod my head ever so slightly. I tighten my lips in a sincere posture. I tell them that “I understand” or “Oh, that must be hard”. I inflect my voice to exaggerate my sincerity. I’ve even put my hand on someone’s arm as a sign of compassion.

During conversations, I actively compassionately listen, however I never lose sight of my tactical advantage. I didn’t know this guy, or whether he had a gun under his jacket, so I spoke to him maintaining my tactical advantage. I realize people just wanted to be heard. They want to tell his side of the story even though there was nothing I can do about it. That is what being a police officer for a local community is all about.

I could of have walked into the back, barked out orders to the man and told him to beat it? I could have done that, but that is exactly what the problem patrolman would have done. This approach would have got the job done, but it would have been at the expense of a mans’ feelings and that would not be right. My overall objective as a police officer is to effectively get the job done with the least amount of friction and the least amount of negative effects. One major concern is determining what type of communication negatively affects which type of people. For example, using the above example, the embrace around the shoulders of the man yielded positive results, however if he was a woman, she may have responded a little differently. Some characteristics to be cognizant of are race, gender, sexual preference, religion, age or even generation.

In today's American culture, everybody has an equal voice and is less accepting of blind leadership. Generation X-ers don't just want to know what to do we want to know why we need to do it. Thus, every future generation wants more information then the previous. So we, as patrolman of society, need to adapt to the new culture, we can't expect the culture to adapt to us. This becomes very important when it comes to managing the new generation of police officers.

The other branch of communication is the actual act of speaking. Speaking is different from talking. Anybody can talk. Talking consists of slang, nonsense, insults, swears or whatever else comes from ones mouth. Speaking is the act of choosing the right words and the correct sentence pattern to make a valid, intelligent argument or statement. The good patrolman knows when to speak, what to say and how to say it. He knows how to ask questions a victim or suspect in a way that does not patronize or insult them. For example, asking the question "Do you go to school" is very different from "Are you currently enrolled in school". Both ask the same question, but the latter is less derogatory. "Do you go to school" implies that one is incapable or not intelligent enough to apply himself to a curriculum. The latter question spares him his feels, and provides him the opportunity to offer a less embarrassing response. His response to the question "Are you currently enrolled in school" could be "well, I took the year off to work and earn some money for next years tuition". This approach is invaluable when building a rapport in an attempt to gain information or maximizing cooperation, and minimizing the threat of physical attack.

The most important benefit of having effective communication skills is it will save a police officers' life. The question I use to illustrate why this skill is important is 'Can I convince him not to kill me?' He, again, is used to describe a police officer's adversary. A good police officer can answer this question by communicating or even attempting to communicate with an adversary. The majority of incidents, especially on television, end in police officers too quickly jumping into physical action when it isn't necessary. Sometimes just speaking and actively listening to someone is the tool you can use to complete the task at hand, maximize effectiveness and avoid an altercation.

III. Defensive self-preservation
The mechanics and tactical actions on how to

keep you safe will be covered in the police academy and other types of self defense trainings. The most important self preservation techniques are discussed in the "Defensive Tactics" chapter of this guide. What I will review in this section is a new perspective regarding the importance of self preservation and how to approach it without pushing the panic button.

The first facet of protecting oneself is image. If a police officer presents himself in a professional manner he will project the perception that he is well trained and ready for anything. In short if you look like you know what you're doing people will think you know what you're doing. There are several ways to properly present yourself. The most obvious way is an officers uniform. If your shirt is tucked in and neat, shoes clean, hair neatly combed and clean shaved you will give a positive image. Most people picture this in their minds when they think of the police. Anything that strays from this norm is considered, by the layperson, as unacceptable. Therefore, if you present yourself in this manner you will be meeting the public's' expectations. For example, if a police officer responds to you home with gravy stains on his shirt, his hair sticking straight up and stubble from a five o'clock shadow on his face, you would ask yourself, 'is this guy kidding me?' The officer may be a completely competent, skilled, street-smart cop, however you would have no confidence that this officer will be able to help you.

Another way to present yourself in a professional manner is your ability to keep your cool under pressure. A citizen calls the police not to talk about how well their day is going, but to report how they are in trouble and need help immediately. When the average citizen is panicking and losing control over a situation they call the police and expect them to show up and regain control. For example, if a gunman walks into a bank and begins shooting innocent victims, witnesses and bystanders call the police. And when everybody is running out, we have to run in. If the police were to panic, run and hide in a tree we would not be fulfilling our obligation.

NOTES

Made in the USA
Lexington, KY
10 July 2018